OBJECT LESSONS

Teaching Math Through the Visual Arts, K–5

Caren Holtzman and Lynn Susholtz

![S]

Stenhouse Publishers
Portland, Maine

Stenhouse Publishers
www.stenhouse.com

Credits
Book
Page 13: "Stolen Generations Accept Apology from Kevin Rudd on Sorry Day." Photo by Lisa Maree Williams. Getty Images News Collection, #79730663. Used with permission of Getty Images.

Pages 13 and 22: "Abraham Obama" used by permission of the artist, Ron English. © 2008 Ron English. www.popaganda.com.

Page 66: *Archaeology* cover used with permission. *Archaeology*: 1988, Vol. 41, No. 1. © Archaeological Institute of America.

"Bonampak Mural, Room 1" © President and Fellows of Harvard College, Peabody Museum of Archaeology and Ethnology, 48-63-20/17559. Used with permission, courtesy of the Peabody Museum of Archaeology and Ethnology.

Page 78: "The Bear" by Tim Hawkinson, from the Stuart Collection at the University of California, San Diego. Photo by Philipp Scholz Rittermann. Copyright © 2005. Reproduced with permission of the University of California, San Diego.

Page 105: "Red Stone" by Elizabeth Murray, from the Stuart Collection at the University of California, San Diego. Photo by Philipp Scholz Rittermann. Copyright © 1996. Reproduced with permission of the University of California, San Diego.

CD
Grids and Graph Paper:
Archaeology cover used with permission. *Archaeology*: 1988, Vol. 41, No. 1. © Archaeological Institute of America.

"Bonampak Mural, Room 1" © President and Fellows of Harvard College, Peabody Museum of Archaeology and Ethnology, 48-63-20/17559. Used with permission, courtesy of the Peabody Museum of Archaeology and Ethnology.

The Rock:
"Zen stone garden at the Komyozenji temple in Dazaifu, Fukuoka prefecture": This Wikipedia and Wikimedia Commons image is from the user Chris 73 and is freely available at http://commons,wikimedia.org/wiki/File:Komyozenji_Stone_garden_1.JPG under the creative commons cc-by-sa 3.0 license.

"The Bear" by Tim Hawkinson, from the Stuart Collection at the University of California, San Diego. Photo by Philipp Scholz Rittermann. Copyright © 2005. Reproduced with permission of the University of California, San Diego.

"Red Stone" by Elizabeth Murray, from the Stuart Collection at the University of California, San Diego. Photo by Philipp Scholz Rittermann. Copyright © 1996. Reproduced with permission of the University of California, San Diego.

Library of Congress Cataloging-in-Publication Data
Holtzman, Caren, 1962–
    Object Lessons : Teaching Math Through the Visual Arts, K–5 / Caren Holtzman and Lynn Susholtz.
        pages cm
    Includes bibliographical references and index.
    ISBN 978-1-57110-796-1 (alk. paper)—ISBN 978-1-57110-893-7 1. Art in mathematics education. 2. Mathematics—Study and teaching (Elementary) I. Susholtz, Lynn, 1957– II. Title. III. Title: Teaching Math Through the Visual Arts, K–5.
    QA19.A78H65 2011
    372.7—dc22

                                        2010041820

Cover design, interior design, and typesetting by Martha Drury

Manufactured in the United States of America
PRINTED ON 30% PCW RECYCLED PAPER

17 16 15 14 13 12 11   9 8 7 6 5 4 3 2 1

Caren dedicates this book to her parents and thanks them for all their help and support.

Lynn dedicates this book to her parents and thanks them for providing a vibrant aesthetic education.

CONTENTS

ACKNOWLEDGMENTS

We'd like to thank Toby Gordon for all her support and insight. Her patience and vision kept us on track and built a foundation for sharing ideas and activities. We're also grateful for the staff and technical support we received from the folks at Stenhouse.

We're indebted to our colleagues and friends who opened their classrooms to us and our project:

Emily Adamick
Central Elementary School
National School District

Sanjana Bryant
Learning Without Limits Elementary School
Oakland Unified School District

Yen Dang
El Toyon Elementary School
National School District

Camie Dyess
Kipp Adelante Charter School
San Diego

Sharon Fargason
Fay Elementary School
San Diego

Elisabeth Frausto
Florence Elementary School
San Diego

Kristin Komatsubara
High Tech Middle Charter School
San Diego

Frances MacKenzie
Florence Elementary School
San Diego

Elizabeth McEvoy
El Toyon Elementary School
National School District

Kathrina Mendoza
Central Elementary School
National School District

Lila Murphy
Florence Elementary School
San Diego

Tina Rasori
Fay Elementary School
San Diego

Danielle Zdunich
McKinley Elementary School
San Diego

And thanks to the University of California–San Diego undergraduates and student teachers who observed, field-tested, and provided invaluable feedback:

Tina Ahmed
Jennifer An
Bayley Aronson
Jed Banayat
Jessica Banuelos

Priscilla Barcellos
Leslie Barnes
Renee Basaez
Vivi-Anna Bergson
Alison Black
Alejandra Burt
Kate Campbell
Cynthia Caputo
Nathalie Carrier
Kelly Chao
Karen Chau
Vivian Chen
Christine Cheng
Annie Chii
Bailey Choi
Jocelyn Chow
Jamie Chu
Tessa Clausen
Jennifer Cole-Regis
Ashley Collins
Christopher Craven
Kelly Christianson
Marissa Curtis
Katherine Czujko
Kellye Daffron
Doris Dave
Melissa D'ooge
Marissa Funk
Nichole Grieco
Georgia Hall
Jillian Haney
Jessica Hawkins
Margaret Hayes
Ben Hinchman
Diana Holland
Rebecca Holland
Jessica Hunt
Elizabeth Irvine-McDermott
Michelle Jimenez
Sarah Kasavan
Mary Kim
Terri Kim
Olivia Kimble
Anjali Kumar
Catherine Kunisch
Alessandra Laetsch
Tiffany Larsen
Sandra Leu
Scott Luong

Natalie Martinez
Misty Mudd
Jessica Newkirk
Vanessa Oram-Solomon
Karen Ong
Elliot Page
Rebekah Painter
Erica Parker
Annie Petterson
Nancy Sandoval
Jennifer Santos
Sarah Serna
Sarah Shulenberger
Christine Sullivan
Emily Sullivan
Adam Stone
Proud Sukthavorn
Adrienne Thompson
Kimberly Tsai
Alexis Turner
Annie Utley
Jaclyn Vasko
Pamelah Walker
Melissa Ward
Jocelyn White
Madelyn Wudel
Winnie Yu
Ginger Yuen
Myrna Zhang

INTRODUCTION

The first thing to understand is that mathematics is an art.
—Paul Lockhart (2009)

Welcome to *Object Lessons*. This book and CD represent the work we've been doing together for more than a decade. We have a unique combined skill set: Caren has ten years of experience as an elementary classroom teacher and is currently a math educator working primarily with preservice and inservice teachers. Lynn has more than twenty years of experience as an art teacher and a working artist. She also directs an art gallery and works on many community-based public art projects.

Together we've worked with thousands of elementary students. The more we collaborated on activities and projects, the more we noticed similarities between art and math processes. We began an ongoing discussion about the links between art and math and came to realize that art is an effective and striking way to highlight core mathematical concepts and processes. The more we talked and worked together, the more we realized how much math and art have in common and how visual art offers a pathway to deep mathematical understanding. We also confirmed how valuable math skills are to real-world art applications.

At first glance, math and art may appear to be very different, very separate subjects. However, we found that visual arts and mathematics share many essential features. Both subjects focus on thinking and problem solving. Mathematicians and artists use their prior knowledge and experiences to explore and investigate new ideas and circumstances. Flexibility and tackling problems from different perspectives allow both mathematicians and artists to solve problems while building a repertoire of skills and knowledge that can be applied to other situations. In addition, effective communication is essential in both fields, as part of the process and as a reason to share the work with others.

Object Lessons is our effort to show the links between math and art, and, more important, to show how visual art can be used to teach core math curriculum in an effective and meaningful way. The visual nature of mathematics is often lost in traditional symbolic and procedure-based mathematics instruction. Our students lose opportunities for problem solving, developing spatial abilities, and making sense of mathematical ideas. Integrating visual arts into math experiences makes the lessons more active, visual, and meaningful. Our students become more focused, competent mathematicians through their visual investigations.

In addition, we found that integrating math with visual art encourages multiple perspectives and avenues of access, supporting engagement and understanding. It deepens and personalizes the learning experience. Teachers and students get an opportunity to value and appreciate each individual's work. This perspective on math opens the classroom to vibrant discussions, enthusiastically shared work, and equitable participation by all members of the classroom community.

We understand that math time might not always feel like an artistic endeavor, but we have found some relatively easy ways to move in that direction. By explicitly combining visual arts and mathematics experiences, teachers and students can share problems and experiences that bring together the visual elements of mathematics and the mathematical elements of visual arts.

This book has three overarching goals:

1. To provide math teachers with a more visual/spatial approach to teaching all areas of math
2. To show ways to integrate visual arts activities into the math curriculum
3. To familiarize math teachers with basic visual arts concepts and vocabulary

In support of these goals, the book offers rich mathematical activities that focus on common objects. These objects become the subject of mathematical and artistic investigation. The objects—flags, shoes, paper, rocks, faces, food, grids, and journals—remind students and teachers that math and art are part of the everyday world. We also want to make these activities easy to implement. We know teachers probably don't have a lot of extra time to plan elaborate lessons requiring exotic materials and arduous preparation. Therefore, we chose common objects as the focus and the primary materials to ensure simplicity and access for all.

We are grateful to the many teachers who tried these activities in their classrooms with their students. Our teacher colleagues provided feedback and shared their students' work to help make this book practical, user-friendly, and academically worthwhile. We shared many of these teachers' descriptions, suggestions, and student work samples to illustrate the power of teaching mathematics through the visual arts. The teachers who field-tested the activities confirm that the lessons can be done easily and with great success.

We hope this book also shows that using visual arts to teach mathematics is fun. Fun is not just an added bonus: it's a key component of learning and being in school. We (teachers and students) need to be motivated and engaged in our school lives. In fact Steven Wolk (2008, 14) implores teachers to "strive in whatever ways they can to own their teaching so that each morning they can enter their classrooms knowing there will be golden opportunities for them—as well as for their students—to experience the joy in school." Exploring mathematics through art unlocks opportunities for such joy.

THE MATH

The mathematics presented within these pages is not watered down in any way. In fact the lessons feature rigorous, high-level mathematics. All the activities address key mathematics standards, skills, and concepts as described by the National Council of Teachers of Mathematics (1989). The lessons also align with the new Common Core State Standards for Mathematics (2010) for mathematical practice and mathematical content.

Students, and certainly teachers, have no time to waste on silly frills. Math is a core subject, a focus of standards and standardized tests, and a high-stakes subject. Success in mathematics determines students' opportunities in the STEM (science, technology, engineering, math) fields. Is this a test prep curriculum? Of course not. Will helping students deepen their understanding of math and giving them visual tools to picture math concepts serve them well on tests? Of course. By concentrating the math content on numbers and operations, geometry, algebra, measurement, and data analysis, the activities slice into the core of the mathematics curriculum. The focus on math practices such as visualizing, sense-making, reasoning, communication, and using mathematical models and tools supports students in developing the requisite mathematical habits of mind.

This methodology provides equitable access to many learners who often check out of math class when they experience it only as a rote, procedural endeavor. The work is real, relevant, interesting, and unpredictable. The products vary; there are no set responses to the challenges presented in perceiving and creating visual models and connecting them to important mathematics.

This approach to mathematics also serves students well beyond the elementary classroom. Students need to be prepared for the complex, interconnected problems and challenges that await them in higher education, the workforce, and the real world in general. Professor Temple Grandin (2009, 253) notes, "I see all kinds of problems with students who have never had an art class or built anything themselves. This lack of hands-on experience really hurts their understanding of how things relate to each other in the physical world." Actively using visual arts to uncover mathematics addresses these concerns.

Furthermore, math is essential to the future of individuals and U.S. society as a whole. Students who find the beauty in mathematics and see it as an interesting and meaningful endeavor continue to pursue the subject. These students with interest and confidence in their ability to do mathematics have access to STEM (science, technology, engineering, math) careers. These are some of the most lucrative and important careers in today's world.

Our students need both skills and creativity to successfully navigate the complex and ever-changing modern world. In a *New York Times* interview Marc Tucker, president of the National Center on Education and the Economy, asserts, "One thing we know about creativity is that it typically occurs when people who have mastered two or more quite different fields use the framework in one to think afresh about the other" (Friedman 2010). Combining visual arts with math not only supports students' mathematical understanding but also helps them develop their creative thinking abilities and prepares them for the future.

THE ART

The art aspect of this book focuses on key visual arts ideas and is not watered down in the least. Far from cookie-cutter activities or holiday art projects, the art and artists presented here represent the ideas and talents of influential arts thinkers and arts makers. Featuring more than forty artists, the book refers to milestone trends in art history. Most of the artists hail from the contemporary art world, known for provoking fresh looks at familiar subjects. Some of the artists are familiar names, and many are emerging talents who speak to new directions in the art world. By introducing this array of artists we hope to help build a foundation for viewing, understanding, and appreciating contemporary art.

We understand that elementary school teachers may or may not have a strong arts background and may or may not have arts resources and art teachers at their schools. However, even if teachers are not personally comfortable and confident in their art proficiency, they can begin to see visual arts' usefulness as a tool for teaching math. And through that usefulness and the access it gives their students to math content, they can build their own enthusiasm for and knowledge of visual arts. This awareness creates an upward spiral in which teachers continuously grow through their use of art in math class. The teacher's growing comfort with art serves the students. As John Dewey (1934, 148) said, "If we've the experience and awareness of how the arts illuminate life, we'll be able to help our students make those connections."

The activities in this book provide an introduction to the techniques and concepts that concern contemporary artists. All of the methods and ideas that these artists use are available to students. Often the procedures and media are simple, although the products are highly crafted. A real arts education, as well as a real math education, lies ahead.

Another benefit of integrating visual arts into math is that students actually get some art content. Many teachers, schools, and districts have essentially shelved art in favor of more minutes dedicated to "core curriculum"—language arts and math. Students (and all people) need art. Although there may not be time or motivation to dedicate chunks of the school day to pure arts instruction, arts can sneak in the side door by pairing with other subjects. In fact, we hope that visual arts teachers will find this book useful as a model for supporting core subjects.

The lessons described in this book focus on core elementary math content while also exposing students to key arts standards. While engaging their students in rich math lessons, teachers also address National Visual Arts Achievement Standards (1994) such as helping students

- identify connections between the visual arts and other disciplines in the curriculum;
- compare the characteristics of works in two or more art forms that share similar subject matter, historical periods, or cultural context;
- describe ways in which the principles and subject matter of other disciplines taught in the school are interrelated with the visual arts.

Visual art records human development across every culture and time period. The study of art history is the study of human civilization and achievement. David Skorton (2007), president of Cornell University, notes that "the arts and humanities play a vital role in the educational development of students. They keep and convey our cultural heritage while opening us up to other societies and civilizations around the globe. They help us explore what it means to be human, including both the ethical and aesthetic dimensions." The arts and arts education provide connections to essential human experiences.

BOOK FORMAT

The chapters are formatted consistently for ease of use. The only chapter that deviates from the standard format is Chapter 8, "The Journal." Journals offer a system for ongoing math and art investigations, so we describe some journal options for teachers to consider. We suggest that teachers first skim that chapter to determine if journals might be an interesting documentation option to begin the lessons and to use throughout the year. The other chapters follow a basic structure:

General Overview
The "General Overview" section provides a brief introduction to the object of focus. It gives a little background and a few tips about using and procuring the object for classroom endeavors.

Math Connections

The "Math Connections" section provides a rationale for the object's use and its connections to important mathematical content and concepts.

Activity Overview

For ease of use, a matrix lists the chapter's activities by grade level and math content area.

Art Connections

To provide teachers with arts background and references, each chapter has a section that connects the object of focus with relevant artists, styles, periods, and techniques.

Arts Vocabulary

The "Arts Vocabulary" section features a list of art terms that arise in different activities throughout the chapter.

Classroom Activities

Each activity description features several sections, which provide teachers with the basics required for preparing and teaching each lesson. In addition, narrative descriptions and graphics provide a clearer picture of how the lesson actually plays out in a classroom. The parts of each activity description include the following:

> Title
> Grade Level
> Math Content Area
> Math Overview
> Guiding Questions
> Vocabulary
> Materials
> Classroom Narrative

THE CD

The CD that accompanies this book highlights the visual arts elements of the activities and teaching. For each chapter the CD contains color images of student artwork, activity reproducibles, and links to relevant artists and Web sites. There is also a general overview of all the artists referred to in the book and links to their Web sites and works. Some other recommended arts and education links round out the CD's contents.

HOW TO USE THE BOOK

We offer this book as an opportunity to supplement the basic math curriculum or to substitute for parts of it. Teachers may find activities to replace some textbook activities, providing the same math content while adding a visual arts element. Teachers also may choose to provide students with visual arts activities that supplement the more traditional math lessons. Either way, students receive core math instruction with a visual arts connection that brings the math to light and to life.

This book isn't intended as a break from "real math." It's intended as a doorway to real math and real mathematical understanding. Looking at math through a visual arts lens provides a window through which students can view and connect to mathematics. And as Maxine Greene (2001, 60) reminds us, "We will find ourselves making connections, discerning meanings, or coming on new perspectives because of what we have beheld." Through a more visual approach and through connecting activities with visual arts and artists, teachers and students will engage with the meaning, beauty, and art of mathematics.

CHAPTER 1

THE FACE

Anyone who has spent time with children knows they tend toward self-centeredness. This is not an insult, but rather a developmental fact. Why not take advantage of this self-interest by focusing activities on the students themselves? Activities exploring the face can provide rich mathematical and artistic opportunities. And this personal focus adds a dimension of intimacy and relevance that both motivates and intrigues.

THE FACE AND THE MATHEMATICS

The face has it all: number, measurement, size, shape, symmetry, ratio, and proportion. It's a veritable gold mine of math investigations. Using the face and its features to explore mathematical concepts gives students ways to connect those concepts with a familiar and important visual context. The activities described in the following sections give a range of ways the face can be the focus of important mathematical explorations across a variety of math content areas.

ACTIVITY	GRADES	NUMBER AND OPERATIONS	ALGEBRA	GEOMETRY	MEASUREMENT	DATA ANALYSIS AND PROBABILITY
Symmetrical Faces	K–2, 3–5			✓		

Polygon Portraits
  Version 1: Picasso
  Version 2: Construction Paper
  Version 3: Crayon-Resist
  Version 4: Cubism
  Version 5: Measuring
	K–5			✓		

Face Measuring	2–3				✓	
Blind Contour Portraits	3–5	✓		✓		
Photo Portraits	3–5			✓		
Disproportionate Portraits	3–5	✓			✓	
Venn Silhouettes	3–5					✓

One activity in particular, *Polygon Portraits*, makes up a good chunk of this chapter. *Polygon Portraits* proved to be highly motivating and adaptable for any grade level. We present a variety of versions of this activity that approach the mathematics and art in different ways. We hope that by seeing the variations and possibilities on one simple activity, readers will be encouraged and inspired to extend and improvise in their own lesson implementations. In this way teachers themselves engage in the creative processes of innovation and experimentation. As always, the human connection, the interactions required, and, of course, the art in these activities make the mathematics both meaningful and memorable.

THE FACE AND THE ART CONNECTIONS

What is more familiar or unique than the human face? It is the first thing an infant learns to recognize and one of the first things a child attempts to draw. There is hardly an artist throughout history who hasn't used his or her own face for a self-portrait or another's as a subject. The face is one of the easiest objects to recognize, but one of the hardest to really see.

Because the face is so ubiquitous, art teachers often use it to devise ways to challenge their students to alter their ways of seeing, to look at their world (and face) with fresh eyes. Our visual habits tend toward the automatic categorization and completion of an image before we have taken the time to really see it. Much of visual artists' work involves "unlearning" the ways we see, to transform the habits we have developed over the years and refine how we see the world. If we can change the patterns of what we see when we look at faces, we can probably change how we see most things in the world. Many of the activities described in this chapter specifically provide opportunities for students to see the face in new ways.

The work of many artists challenges us to see the face in ways that can both represent universal qualities of humanity and reflect uniquely individual traits. A number of artworks throughout the centuries seem to embody a particular time period, a particular style, or a particular social experience. Think of the *Mona Lisa*, a Cubist portrait by Picasso, or Shepard Fairey's famous poster of President Obama from the 2008 campaign. What better way do we have of visually representing cultural history, a particular style, or a particular social environment than through the artistic representation of the human face?

Many artists use the face exclusively in their work. One of the most well-known and accomplished portrait artists living today is Chuck Close. In painting, printmaking, and photographic media he has been using faces as his primary subject since the early 1970s. Interestingly, the grid is an underlying organizing element in all of his portraits, regardless of which medium he employs. When viewed closely his extremely enlarged portraits show facial features in such exaggerated detail that the viewer sees only abstract shapes and colors. This exaggeration alters the image, making it more impersonal, while allowing viewers to reflect on the subject from their personal experience.

Pablo Picasso's work reflects the stylistic changes and cultural history of Western art in the twentieth century. Picasso, along with Georges Braque and others, pioneered the art movement called Cubism, a stylistic process of seeing and depicting an object from multiple perspectives at once. Cubists deconstructed their subjects, even images of the face, into abstracted geometric shapes. This blending of a familiar image with geometric forms provides a perfect place for math and art to intersect. Children seem naturally attracted to the Cubist style of representation.

Etienne de Silhouette, a French finance minister, made the silhouette or "shadow portrait" popular in the 1700s. The portraits were cut out of black paper and quickly became a favorite of the aristocratic societies in Europe and the United States. The contemporary artist Kara Walker has used the black paper cutout silhouettes as her primary medium since the early 1990s. In her artwork, Walker calls attention to racial and gender stereotypes and issues of historic power and privilege. She has taken an antiquated technique and used it to create room-sized installations that are provocative and engaging visual narratives.

Portrait painting has a long and established history in art. Although it was once reserved for wealthy arts patrons, royalty, and political or religious figures, many contemporary artists have used the tradition of portraiture to honor and glorify everyday people. Today we see a wide range of artists painting people from their own unique personal and cultural perspectives.

Kehinde Wiley is a contemporary artist who creates larger-than-life-sized portraits of media stars, athletes, and young black men in their everyday clothing, usually in front of a richly colored and patterned background. Based on photographs taken on the street or informal studio poses, Wiley's paintings reveal qualities of strength and virtue in these young men that are not often seen represented in our contemporary visual culture.

The Mexican artist Frida Kahlo was famous for her self-portraits. A childhood accident caused her to be confined to bed for years. Her father, a photographer, installed a mirror above her bed. She literally spent years staring at herself and creating self-portraits. She frequently added other objects and animals to them. These items depicted her concerns, her experiences, and her dreams. Critics and artists champion her work, and she ranks as a contemporary cultural icon.

 **Face Art Vocabulary:** Abstract Expressionism, abstraction, asymmetry, contour, Cubism, perspective, portrait, profile, proportion, self-portrait, silhouette, symmetry

THE FACE LESSONS

LESSON | # Symmetrical Faces

Grade Level: | K–2, 3–5

Math Content Area: | Geometry

Math Overview: | In this activity students create two-dimensional symmetrical images. They explore and analyze the geometric attributes of the face while exploring congruence. Students use their spatial sense to approximate the location of various features on one half of the face. They also need to keep the symmetrical balance of the face in mind. When considering their final products, students confront issues of symmetry, proportion, measurement, and perspective.

Guiding Questions: | **K–2**
    What shapes do you see on a face?
    What is symmetry? How can you tell when something is symmetrical?
3–5
    What does *bilateral symmetry* mean?
    What makes a face symmetrical?
    How might you create a symmetrical drawing?

Vocabulary: | symmetrical, congruent, balance, bilateral

Materials: | pictures of faces cut in half vertically; 9-by-12-inch construction or drawing paper; pencils, crayons, colored pencils, or oil pastels

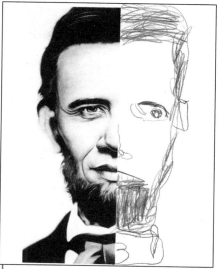
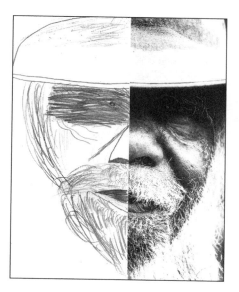

This activity can be done with magazine photos or with 8½ -by-11-inch photos of students' faces. Digital photos of students can be printed out, folded in half vertically, and cut down the middle. Either black-and-white or color photos work for this activity. Glue half of the face photo to one side of a piece of paper. Have students then attempt to complete the portrait by drawing the missing half of the face. Results vary widely, depending on grade level and experience.

This activity is designed to be disorienting and to disrupt the usual way of seeing a subject. It generates interesting discussions and often bears surprising results.

LESSON | Polygon Portraits

Grade Level: K–5

Math Content Area: Geometry

Math Overview: In this activity students use simple shapes to create polygon portraits. The task engages students with the crucial geometric skills of identifying and comparing the attributes of two-dimensional shapes while also seeing how those shapes can be taken apart and recombined to create other shapes.

Guiding Questions:
K–2
    Where are the shapes on the faces?
    What words can you use to tell where they are?
3–5
    How can you combine shapes to create new shapes?
    How might you describe the location and position of shapes on a plane surface?
    How does perspective change when viewing the same object from different angles?

Vocabulary: curved, straight, edge, polygon, regular, irregular, congruent, vertex, vertices, angle, plane

Materials: A list of materials accompanies each version of the activity.

In this activity students can use mirrors to look for polygons in their own faces (as Frida Kahlo did), or they can pair up and do polygon portraits of their partners. The basic structure of the *Polygon Portraits* activity is rather straightforward and is indicated by the name of the activity itself.

1. Students define and list polygons they know. The teacher records the picture and name of each polygon on the board.
2. Connect the use of polygons in art to the style of Cubism.
3. Challenge students to create portraits of themselves or a partner using only polygons. Encourage them to connect their work to the artists and artwork presented.
4. Use the math standards as a guide for assessing and probing for understanding of important geometry concepts.

Although the structure of the activity is quite simple, it can lead into a variety of rich explorations. Following are descriptions of some different versions of the *Polygon Portraits* activity taught in different classrooms.

Polygon Portraits Version 1:
Picasso Polygon Self-Portraits with Oil Pastels

Materials: 9-by-12-inch white construction paper, oil pastels, mirrors

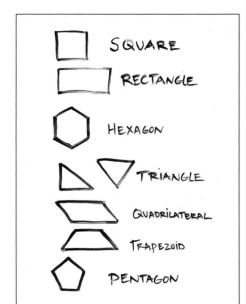

Alexis Turner decided to use Picasso as a jumping-off point for the activity with her third graders. The lesson's math focus was on identifying, describing, and using different polygons. First, students defined the word *polygon.* Then they created a list of polygons and discussed their features.

Alexis also showed some examples of shapes that were not polygons.

Next she introduced Pablo Picasso and showed slides of his portrait paintings to the class. She asked them to share their insights and questions about his work. The slide show of Picasso's art was an essential visual model for students.

The Picasso introduction sparked a conversation about the mixture of geometry and art. Partners shared things they noticed and things they questioned in his art. For instance, the students noticed that Picasso used a lot of colors and lines and wondered how he got his ideas. Alexis guided the discussion toward shapes, Abstract Art, and color use. She distributed mirrors and oil pastels, and the students drew self-portraits using only polygons. The oil pastels created rich, deep colors and could be blended like paint. (This same activity also works well with crayon or colored pencil.) Finally, they needed to describe their portraits using polygon vocabulary and features.

For a final assessment Alexis had the students use these sentence frames to share the different polygons they had used to create their pieces:

In my self-portrait, I used _____ as _____.
_____ have _____ sides and _____ angles.

Alexis asked students to share these sentences with a partner and then asked for volunteers to share their art and their descriptions with the class. She summed up the lesson as follows: "Earlier in the activity when we created a class list of polygon names, some students had difficulty remembering the name of the polygon or the number of sides. They showed progress when they shared at the end of the lesson. They learned and reinforced the names through their verbal and artistic practice. The students were engaged in both the mathematical and artistic sides of the lesson. Not only were students able to draw and show their understanding of polygons through pictures, but they were introduced to Pablo Picasso and his style of art."

To extend the activity Alexis had her students use more specific polygons such as equilateral triangles, parallelograms, and rhombi. She also had students use a minimum number of polygons; for example she told them to use at least six different polygons in their portraits. This challenge prompted the students to stretch themselves by using less familiar polygons.

Polygon Portraits Version 2:
Partner Portraits with Construction Paper Shapes

Materials: construction paper, scissors, glue

Olivia Kimble had her third graders create a variety of "closed, straight-edged shapes" from colored construction paper. Rather than ask them to make self-portraits, Olivia had the students pair up and create portraits of each other. She found that the collaborative structure motivated the students and kept them enthusiastically engaged.

First Olivia led a brainstorming session in which students generated a list of polygons. Once the list was recorded on the board, students set to work cutting the shapes from construction paper. This part of the activity simultaneously reinforced the students' concept of polygons and helped them prepare for the work to come.

Before they got to work on their portraits, many of the students expressed concern that they would not be able to create realistic portraits without curved lines. However, as they worked, many of them expressed their surprise at how appealing their portraits actually were.

When Olivia asked students to brainstorm a list of polygons during the lesson's introduction, many of them could think only of triangles, squares, and other relatively simple examples. However, as they brought their artistic visions to life, many of them began creating polygons of a variety of shapes and sizes, such as parallelograms, trapezoids, hexagons, and pentagons. Olivia worked with the students to help them name these new polygons based on the number of sides and angles. Ultimately, identifying and recognizing the attributes of different polygons was the objective of her lesson, and she was quite pleased to see her students meet it.

Polygon Portraits Version 3:
Crayon-Resist Polygon Portraits

Materials: 9-by-12-inch white construction paper, black crayons, watercolor paints and brushes, cups of water to clean brushes

Diana Holland implemented a different version of *Polygon Portraits* with fourth graders. She had students first use black crayon to create a polygon portrait line drawing of their partner. When the lines were done, students used watercolors to fill in the shapes in their portraits. The wax in crayons resists water so students could paint over the lines without compromising their visibility.

Diana introduced the lesson by starting with polygons. Three students took turns making polygons at the board. They reviewed the rules for polygons (straight lines, closed). Next, two students came to the board. She asked one student to try to find a shape close to a polygon on the other student's face. He chose a triangle to represent her nose. They discussed how artists look at the world in different and interesting ways. When drawing polygon portraits, artists need to find something in their friend's face that they had never seen before. Finally, Diana asked a volunteer to draw her partner's whole face using polygons quickly, in ten seconds. The students found this to be challenging and fun.

After the students had sufficient practice, Diana sent them on their way. Students chose partners, scrutinized one another's faces, drew their partner's portrait with black crayon, and then moved on to watercolors.

Students used their knowledge of geometry to create images of their peers. They attempted to communicate a feeling or personality through their work. Students enjoyed using the polygons to make artwork and learned a great deal about creative expression as well as geometry through this activity.

Polygon Portraits Version 4:
Cubism, Perspective, and Polygon Portraits

Materials: construction paper, scissors, pencils, glue

Jill Haney used the *Polygon Portraits* activity as a context for combining Cubism and geometry in her fifth-grade classroom. She also focused on the idea of perspective and the fact that viewers see different pieces and shapes of the same object, depending on where they are situated.

Jill and the students discussed the use of geometric shapes in Cubism and looked at several examples of Cubist works of art. She introduced the term *Abstract* and discussed its purpose in Cubism, giving some history of the movement. Beginning in the early twentieth century, artists explored abstraction, or the move away from representational imagery. Early Cubists revolutionized Abstract Art when they broke down objects into simple shapes while showing them from multiple perspectives at once. This approach developed into stylistic movements such as Abstract Expressionism in which paintings no longer had discernible imagery, only shapes and colors that represented a feeling or experience.

Next they explored the idea of multiple perspectives. Jill brought student volunteers forward to demonstrate how simple polygons could be used to show their facial features. She asked the student volunteers to turn 90 degrees, and the students reevaluated what they saw and how the shapes changed as the perspective changed. The demonstration made it easy to see the differences in shapes between a frontal view and a side view, or profile, of the student.

After the introduction students went back to their tables, where they had construction paper, scissors, and pencils. Their job was to draw shapes they could see in different people's faces. Then they cut these shapes out and put them together to assemble an abstract portrait of a person, using multiple perspectives.

After students had worked on their abstract portraits, they shared their work and had a whole-class discussion, focusing on the different polygons they had used and what perspectives those polygons represented. Students began to grasp the concept of perspective and were able to make connections between real objects and the shapes they contain.

Many students were surprised to find how much easier art and math could be when broken down into their basic elements. One student said it was strange to see how all those separate shapes could come together to create a picture that resembled a face. Another student said it was neat to see how the same parts of the face looked so different from different angles and that it was fun to use several different perspectives to create something that ended up looking like a face.

The students were very excited and quite proud as they shared their artwork with friends and families at their open house.

Polygon Portraits Version 5:
Polygon Portraits as Measurement Preparation

Materials: | construction paper, scissors, glue, graph paper

Melissa D'ooge used the *Polygon Portraits* activity as a geometry review and to prepare her fifth graders for upcoming lessons about finding the area and perimeter of polygons. She started the lesson by discussing what the students already knew about polygons. First they did a partner talk, and then they did some whole-class sharing. The students were able to name several types of regular polygons. After they shared some ideas, Melissa added words that she thought were important to go over, such as *regular, irregular, congruent, similar, vertex,* and *vertices.*

After discussing polygons and showing examples, they discussed Cubism and Abstract Art. Melissa made a slide show of images and the students viewed the paintings and discussed what they noticed. The students examined art by Pablo Picasso and Georges Braque as well as a sample polygon portrait Melissa had made. Melissa asked the students to talk with partners and list the polygons they noticed. Then, they discussed how the artists depicted certain body parts by using only shapes.

From here, they transitioned into independent work time. Students drew polygon portraits using the shapes and styles they had just discussed. While circulating the room, Melissa saw that almost all students understood the concept of creating a portrait using only polygons. Many wanted to take their portraits home to their parents, showing they were proud of their work.

Melissa found that the students internalized the activity's math concepts. When it came time to work with finding perimeter and area of shapes a week later, they remembered everything from the *Polygon Portraits* experience. They also wanted to make polygon portraits again, this time with graph paper. So Melissa had the students draw portraits on graph paper and then find the area and perimeter of the polygons in their pictures. Clearly the students enjoyed the lesson and transferred important ideas from it to a new situation. Thus the *Polygon Portraits* activity took on new life by serving as a context for measurement practice.

LESSON

Face Measuring

Grade Level: | 2–3

Math Content Area: | Measurement

Math Overview: | In the *Face Measuring* activity, students use rulers to measure and record the length, width, and height of various facial features. Students familiarize themselves with standard units (centimeters) while developing linear measurement skills.

Guiding Questions: | What tools can you use for measuring?
How do you use those measuring tools?

Vocabulary: ruler, centimeter, measure, unit

Materials: rulers, pencils, paper

Winnie Yu had a combined class of second and third graders. The math curriculum required them to learn about centimeters, so she had them practice measuring each other's faces. Winnie paired up her students and had each measure the other's facial features (length and width of mouth, nose, eyes, and ears) using the centimeter side of the ruler. She noted a range of students' proficiency with this task. Some students easily measured and rounded when things weren't exact. Others struggled to place the ruler properly and identify the units on the ruler. It turned out to be both good practice and a good assessment.

Students then tried to transfer their recorded measurements to a portrait drawing. Most of them didn't place the different features properly on the face. For example, many had the eyes too high or the mouth and nose too far apart. These miscalculations made for some interesting portraits and also a follow-up math activity. Winnie introduced the idea of negative space— the space between or around objects. She had students consider the whole face, including both the features and the negative space around and between the features. Students then went back to explore and measure their partner's faces, keeping the features and the space in mind. This awareness also helped them to informally explore some face ratios (distance from top of head to eyes, space between nose and mouth, and distance between eyes). Students used this new information to try to create more proportionally accurate portraits.

LESSON | Blind Contour Portraits

Grade Level: | 3–5

Math Content Area: | Number and Operations, Geometry

Math Overview: | *Blind Contour Portraits* challenge students to consider proportion, ratio, and location of facial features. Fractions serve as benchmarks to help students consider the relative size and position of the features. Students estimate relative size and distance using fractions and apply these estimates to their drawing task.

Guiding Questions: |
Number and Operations
If your face is one whole, what fraction describes the distance from your _____ to your _____? How did you make your estimate?
What fraction describes how far down your face your eyes are?
What ratio approximately describes the relationship between your face length and your face width?
Geometry
What shapes make up a face? What are their relative sizes and locations?

Vocabulary: | line, contour, continuous, shape, space, distance, proportion

Materials: | paper, pencils

An excellent warm-up activity involves having students pair up to make blind contour drawings of each other's faces. Contour lines are the invisible lines that go around a subject, separating it from the background. Contour lines also delineate features inside objects. This activity is called a *blind* contour drawing because students create the contour drawing without looking at their paper at all. They are allowed to look only at their subject. Students are challenged to really see their subject while not being able to see the results of their work until they're finished. This makes the process as much fun as the product. And the products are truly delightful and creative.

Introduce the activity by talking about proportions and spatial relationships on a face. Upper-elementary students benefit from thinking about the face in terms of fractions and proportions. Ask students to generate their own fraction or ratio statements about their faces.

Emphasize the approximating nature of these tasks. The focus on estimation rather than accuracy helps students develop their number sense and also serves to minimize the differences in individual face ratios. Correct answers are not the point here. The goal is for students to notice the details of the face and the relationships between the features. Once students have some spatial sense of the face and its features, introduce the *Blind Contour Portraits* assignment.

1. Pair up.
2. Draw your partner's face for five minutes. You must look only at your partner's face—not the paper. You must keep your pencil on the paper; your drawing will be one continuous line.

It helps to remind students that five minutes can feel like a very long time and that they should try to go very slowly, really looking at and drawing every detail. Urge them to try to remember where they are and what they have already drawn, and to think ahead about where to start on their papers. Younger students might start with a two-minute drawing time frame.

Discussions arise from the products themselves. Ask students what was challenging about this task. Have them compare their blind contour drawings with the actual faces. What is the same? What is different? Where did they start their drawing? Encourage the use of math and art vocabulary in these discussions. Emphasize the importance of spatial awareness and planning in this activity.

LESSON | Photo Portraits

Grade Level: 3–5

Math Content Area: Geometry

Math Overview: *Photo Portraits* allow students to investigate the results of subdividing and rotating images. Students attempt to create pictures similar to the one they're provided with, which forces them to analyze the attributes of shapes and estimate the distance between shapes on a plane. Because students use an upside-down image, they practice spatial visualizing and predicting the results of moving objects on a plane.

Guiding Questions: What happens when shapes are subdivided, combined, flipped, or rotated? What stays the same? What changes?

Vocabulary: vertical, fourth, flip

Materials: photographs or copies of photos of faces (from magazines or any other source); paper, pencils, crayons, colored pencils, or oil pastels

The *Photo Portraits* activity is another effective introductory activity that forces students to really study the features of a face rather than just draw their idea of a face. Have students fold a picture of a face in quarters vertically so the face is divided into four long rectangles. Then have them fold the picture back on itself so that only the first fourth of the face is showing.

Finally, tell them to turn the picture upside down. From here have students attempt to re-create what they see on a blank piece of paper. Upon completion of the first fourth, students unfold the picture to reveal the next upside-down fourth. They continue to draw that portion of the picture on their paper until they've drawn the whole picture from its upside-down image.

When they are finished, students can color their portraits using crayons, colored pencils, or oil pastels. Emphasize the mathematics of the activity by asking them to compare the original photo with their rendition of it. How did flipping the image affect their work? Where did they start? Which shapes changed as a result of the flipping?

LESSON

Disproportionate Portraits

Grade Level: 3–5

Math Content Areas: Number and Operations, Measurement

Math Overview: *Disproportionate Portraits* give students practice with linear measurement. Students also use multiplication and fractions to alter some of their measurements and consider the resulting skewed images. Students tackle issues of proportion, balance, and magnitude through this engaging task.

Guiding Questions:

Number and Operations
What happens to a _____ when one dimension is doubled or halved?
Measurement
How might you measure irregular shapes?

Vocabulary: proportion, double, half, circle

Materials: colored construction paper, rulers, white 9-by-12-inch construction paper, scissors, glue, *Disproportionate Portraits* recording sheet (see appendix and CD)

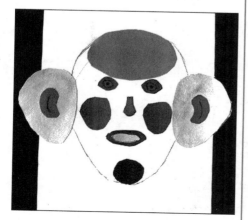

In this activity students pair up and measure each other's facial features. They use the recording sheet to keep track of their work. After they've recorded the measurements, they pick one feature to double and record the doubled measurement. Then they pick a different feature to halve. They record the halved measurement on the recording sheet as well.

When they have completed the measuring tasks, they use the data on their recording sheets to create a portrait of their partner. First they draw an outline of their partner's face on white construction paper. Using the measurements previously collected, they draw the features on different-colored pieces of construction paper. Then they cut out the features and glue them to the white paper to make a portrait collage. These collages, by design, will not look like the actual subject. This makes the activity low-stakes, nonthreatening fun, and mathematically rich.

LESSON

Grade Level:

Math Content Areas:

Math Overview:

Guiding Questions:

Vocabulary:

Materials:

Venn Silhouettes

3–5

Data Analysis and Probability

Venn Silhouettes offer students the chance to collect data and compare different ways to represent it. Students ask questions and draw conclusions based on the data generated. These ideas then become a springboard for further data collection and data analysis opportunities.

How can you gather information about yourself and others?
How can you display that data in a clear way?
What predictions can you make based on the data you collected?

Venn diagram, silhouette, overlap, same, different, compare, contrast, survey, graph, certain, equally likely, unlikely, impossible, profile

overhead projector, large pieces of newsprint or butcher paper, pencils, markers, tape

This activity generates really great posters that can be used to explore data and probability. To get started, students pair up. (Three students can also team up to create a three-variable Venn. They just need to make sure each silhouette partially overlaps the other two.) Students tape a large piece of paper to the wall across from the overhead projector. They need to check to make sure the

projector light is hitting the paper directly. Then one student needs to sit or stand between the overhead and the paper so that the shadow of his or her profile is visible on one side of the paper, covering about half the space. The partner traces around the shadow to outline the silhouette. Next the partners switch. The student who first drew now sits or stands between the overhead and the paper, facing the opposite direction, and his or her silhouette is projected onto the paper so it partly overlaps the existing outline.

Thus a silhouette Venn diagram is created. Partners then get together and discuss things they have in common and things that are unique to each of them. They use colored markers to record their common traits in the overlapping section of the Venn silhouette. They record their unique traits with symbols and words in their respective nonoverlapping sections. These colorful, visual, personal products look great posted on bulletin boards and provide an unusual way for students to get to know each other at the beginning of the school year.

Once this personal data is sorted on the Venn diagram, teachers can have their students pursue several different math paths. To emphasize probability, post the Venn silhouettes around the room and have students do a gallery walk. Students can use this experience to expand their ideas about what information they can put on their silhouettes. They might also begin to notice some commonalities and some unusual information about their classmates. These observations trigger questions and "I wonder" statements. For example, students might wonder how many classmates have a younger sister or how many have ever been out of the country. These questions then become survey questions. Students pick a question that interests them and collect data from the entire class. They create different types of graphs (bar, line, T-table) to display their findings about the class.

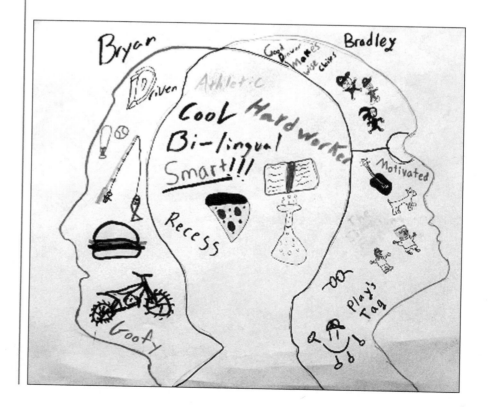

Another probability extension entails having partners pair up with another pair to share their Venn silhouettes. They observe and discuss what they notice about the data. From there they use the data from their two Venn silhouettes to make predictions about the rest of the class. Providing sentence frames and prompts helps focus the students on important probability vocabulary and concepts.

We predict that in our class . . .
it is certain that _____.
it is likely that _____.
it is unlikely that _____.
it is impossible that _____.

From here, students can create surveys based on their predictions and collect data from classmates. They can make posters about and/or graph their survey results. They can also write about whether their predictions matched the actual class data and hypothesize about the possible reasons. In addition, they might make predictions about the entire grade level or school based on the data from their surveys.

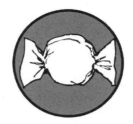

CHAPTER 2

FOOD

Motivating? You bet! Who doesn't like food? And it's always a special treat to have food in the classroom. Today we see a renewed interest in food. Public discussions about food and nutrition, sustainable agriculture, school gardens, healthful lunches, and food equity feature prominently on TV and in print media. Several television channels are devoted solely to programming about food. It seems we are rediscovering the connections between food, health, economy, and community. Food is never far from our hearts, minds, and stomachs. It is a perfect way to make connections to every area of the curriculum.

A few caveats or acknowledgments before we go any further: There are compelling reasons why some teachers don't like to use food in their classrooms. Management can be an issue. Students get excited, and their initial burning question—"Can we eat it?"—can overwhelm any other features of the activity. Some students have food allergies and it's safer not to introduce things into the environment that might trigger a health problem. If students are ultimately going to eat the food, we need to consider hygiene

ACTIVITY	GRADES	NUMBER AND OPERATIONS	ALGEBRA	GEOMETRY	MEASUREMENT	DATA ANALYSIS AND PROBABILITY
Cerealscapes	K–2	✓	✓			
Potato and Apple Stamping	K–2		✓			
Polygon Fruit Bowl Still Life	K–2			✓		
Polyhedra Food Sculptures	2–5			✓		
Pasta and Pipe-Cleaner Playgrounds	3–5	✓		✓	✓	
Candy Block Sculptures	3–5	✓		✓	✓	
Candy Block Patterns	3–5		✓			
Bean and Seed Mosaics	3–5	✓		✓	✓	

and contamination. Students need to wash their hands, not share food, and have a clean place to put the food.

Should you choose not to use food in your classroom, you still might benefit from skimming this chapter. Some of the activities can be accomplished with nonfood items. You might substitute Plasticine or modeling clay for marshmallows or gumdrops, or substitute small, different-shaped nonfood items for cereal, beans, or seeds.

The decision to use food needs to be considered carefully. That said, we weighed the pros and cons and said, "Let's go for it!" The students delighted us with their ability to restrain themselves, adhere to the established rules and guidelines, and focus on the activities rather than the materials. Being explicit about behavioral expectations always makes an activity run more smoothly, and this is especially true when using food. We acknowledged to the students that although they might be tempted to eat the food, it was to be used for a math and art investigation, not for a snack. One successful approach was letting students know that we had some extra food that they could eat when the activity was over. That way, they knew they would eventually get to eat a treat and didn't have to worry about hoarding or sneaking bites during the activity.

We also emphasized the health and germ aspect of the endeavor. The food we were using for the math and art activities was going to be touched, breathed on, and sneezed on by a lot of people, plus it would be on top of dirty desks. It was definitely not desirable to ingest it. In fact, it would be kind of gross!

FOOD AND THE MATHEMATICS

Math is a key ingredient in food. Recipes almost always involve measurement and fractions. They often involve doubling and halving. Foods are full of shape and volume. Even the packaging of food is full of mathematical information—weight, size, calories, percentages, and price. Many word problems in traditional textbooks involve food. You get your pizza fractions, your candy sharing, your converting quarts of milk to liters. These contrived word problems lack the interaction and immediacy that characterizes our real dealings with food. The ideas described in this chapter take food off the worksheet and put it onto the tabletop. Here students use food and food contexts to explore many important mathematical concepts and problems.

FOOD AND THE ART CONNECTIONS

Some of the oldest expressions of art involve the depiction of food with artists painting scenes of hunting, farming, and feasting. In every region of the world we find depictions of food carved on ceramic containers, tools, friezes, and ancient artifacts. Food is our cultural common denominator, essential to all life. Regional and ritual foods feature prominently in almost all cultural and religious festivals.

An Internet search yields thousands of images of "food art." Sculpted and collaged foodstuff can make for some amazing creations. Artists produce carvings made from butter, chocolate, and cheese; mosaics of pasta, beans, and candy; and clothes made from meat. Egg tempera is a paint medium still used by artists today. Many museums dedicate themselves to food: museums of burned food, soul food, sugar, root beer, and chocolate. The list goes on.

Contemporary Art (a term used to describe artworks created after World War II) encompasses a wide range of media used to depict food. Food is rich in symbolism. Artists use images of food to represent personal experience, cultural history, and political and social issues. There are several contemporary artists known for paintings or sculptures of food. Many Pop artists employed food as a subject for its symbolic resonance with commercial society and the rapidly evolving modern culture of the 1960s.

Food itself is used as a medium for artworks. In this chapter we introduce sculptures, mosaics, and landscapes created with food. The *Polyhedra Food Sculptures* and *Pasta and Pipe-Cleaner Playgrounds* activities have connections to architecture, art, and industrial design. Whether considered design, art, or engineering, creative problem solving is at the heart of these activities.

Buckminster Fuller was a creative problem-solver who considered physical structures from both engineering and aesthetic perspectives. Fuller was an architect, designer, and inventor. Born in Massachusetts in 1895, he was an early environmentalist and advocate of what he termed "*design science*—a systematic study of the deliberate ordering of the components in our universe." Fuller explained, "The function of what I call design science is to solve problems by introducing into the environment new artifacts, the availability of which will induce their spontaneous employment by humans and thus, coincidentally, cause humans to abandon their previous problem-producing behaviors and devices" (Fuller and Kuromiya 1992, 52).

Considered a futurist for his interest in human ecosystems and innovative approaches to everything from harnessing sustainable energy sources to designing alternative communities, Fuller was most famous for popularizing the geodesic dome, a spherical structure made of adjacent triangles capable of holding a great amount of weight compared with its mass. Buckminster Fuller's ideas and inventions continue to influence and inspire students of both arts and sciences. His approach to design and problem solving helps students consider their own work in creating various food structures in this chapter.

Alexander Calder's work connects well with some of the food construction activities described here. Calder worked primarily in metal, creating objects that range in size from small jewelry pieces to monumental steel sculptures. A contemporary of Fuller's, Calder originally studied to become an engineer. A prolific artist throughout his career, his sculptures include abstract "mobiles" (kinetic, or moving objects), "stabiles" (nonkinetic sculptures), wire portraits, and cast bronze sculptures. In the early 1920s Calder was an illustrator for a newspaper in New York, which assigned him to sketch scenes from the circus. After that he began his much celebrated series of mobiles, stabiles, and interactive wire sculptures of circus performers and animals. Calder played with balance and movement in his work. His wire sculptures and portraits are wondrous feats of creating lifelike drawings with bent wire. They are a delicate balance both visually and physically.

Landscapes (seascapes and skyscapes) have a long history as a pictoral genre. Referring to a two-dimensional representation view of a natural environment, landscape scenes have been depicted in every kind of media. Aerial photographers, impressionist painters, and traditional Japanese woodblock printers have all used landscape as their source material. There are many different ways to depict landscapes. A landscape scene can be a realistic representation of a vista or an imaginary backdrop for objects. This chapter includes an activity that uses food as the primary material for creating imaginary landscapes.

Masterful painter Wayne Thiebaud began using food as a subject early in his career. He studied commercial art in college and began working as a sign painter and cartoonist after spending one summer working at the Walt Disney studios. While working in a café he became interested in images of production-line food at diners and cafeterias. His technique of building up thick and luscious layers of oil paint perfectly expresses both the tactile and emotional qualities attached to food. His voluptuous paintings of cakes, pies, and candy are almost as enjoyable as the real thing. Thiebaud received the National Medal of Arts in 1994.

Claes Oldenburg first began creating his "soft sculptures" in the early 1960s. These oversized humorous replicas of everyday objects were made of stuffed fabric. He created hundreds of sculptures of all kinds of objects, including hamburgers, ice-cream cones, and slices of cake. His drawings and giant sculptures of everyday objects, such as a Popsicle or a stuffed potato for a public plaza, reflect the playfulness and humor in his work. He received many commissions with his wife, Coosje van Bruggen, to create sculptures for public spaces all over the world. Encountering the unexpected scale of these sculptures is both delightful and thought-provoking. Can we see something as familiar as an ice-cream cone in a fresh new way by changing its size and material? Might we reconsider the role of commerce in food production when viewing food as art?

Carmen Lomas Garza paints and writes children's books, including *Family Pictures/Cuadros de Familia* and *In My Family/En Mi Familia*. She paints pictures of the life events from her childhood growing up in south Texas. Her work tells a story about family and culture through the depiction of the use of everyday objects. Many of her paintings and prints incorporate images of food being prepared and shared. In *Tamalada*, *Sandía*, *Nopalitos*, and *Barbacoa Para Cumpleaños*, food becomes a central focus of the painting. Garza's work is in the collection of the Smithsonian American Art Museum.

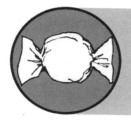

Food Art Vocabulary: background, foreground, kinetic, landscape, mobile, perspective, sculpture, seascape, shape, skyscape, stabile, still life, three-dimensional, two-dimensional, volume

THE FOOD LESSONS

LESSON | Cerealscapes

Grade Level: K–2

Math Content Area: Number and Operations, Algebra

Math Overview: *Cerealscapes* combine an important art form—the landscape—with fundamental math concepts for primary students. Estimating, counting, grouping, and sorting all appear during the activity. Students engage their number sense, display their skills with counting and adding, and connect concrete materials to standard mathematical notation.

Guiding Questions:

Number and Operations
How many pieces of cereal did you use?
How did you find the total?
Algebra
Can you sort or group your cereal to make it easier to count?
What's the connection between the addition equation and the groups you made?

Vocabulary: landscape, seascape, skyscape, background, foreground, addition, total

Materials: 9-by-12-inch construction paper (blue, green, black, brown), crayons, various shapes of dry cereal (we used Cheerios, Honeycomb, Chex, Froot Loops, and Lucky Charms), *Cerealscapes Recording Sheet* (see appendix and CD)

Emily Adamick allowed us to bring some food, art, and math to her first-grade classroom. To start the lesson we wrote the words *Landscape, Seascape*, and *Skyscape* on the board and asked students what words they noticed inside these bigger words. The students identified the connection to land, sea, and sky.

Then we showed the students a slide show of different landscapes, seascapes, and skyscapes. They named the objects they saw in each, and we recorded the items on the board under the appropriate heading. This list would provide students with ideas for their pictures when they worked independently. After they had viewed the slide show, we asked the students to brainstorm a few other ideas for the list. We wanted to encourage their creativity and make sure the subsequent part of the activity would be as open as possible. We accomplished our mission. The board showed a nice mix of ideas in each category.

Landscape	Seascape	Skyscape
house	rocks	bird
tree	boat	sun
grass	mega-mouth shark	cloud
flowers	octopus	butterfly
reptile	blue whale	airplane
car	seaweed	rain

We then told the students that they were going to create their own art piece. We instructed them to decide if they wanted to make a land-, sea-, or skyscape and to identify two objects they wanted to feature in their piece. They chose a background color of green, blue, brown, or black construction paper and used a pencil to draw an outline of their two objects on the paper. We encouraged them to draw big and fill the paper as much as they could. We modeled the process briefly on the board before sending them off to work.

Before distributing cereal to the tables we had a brief but important talk about its proper use. Then we gave them a variety of cereals (Cheerios, Honeycomb, Chex, Froot Loops, and Lucky Charms) to use to cover their artwork. Students were very receptive and had excellent control over themselves and the materials throughout the lesson.

When students finished covering their pictures with cereal, they raised their hand so we could take a photo of their masterpieces. We decided to take photos rather than have the students glue the cereal permanently onto the paper for two reasons. First, we wanted students to be able to sort and count the cereal, and we thought they would be better able to do this if they could physically manipulate the pieces. We also believed that gluing cereal would be cumbersome and messy. The photos allowed us to save the student work even after they removed the cereal. Emily posted the photos in a gallery on the class Web site, meaning the artwork was able to gain a wider audience.

We focused on math by having students quantify the cereal they used. We provided a recording sheet to tell how much of each type they used and how many pieces they used altogether.

The math was very rich and appropriate for the first graders. Students used a variety of approaches to count and add their cereal pieces. Some had a difficult time sorting and counting, whereas others breezed through this job. Asking students to explain or show how they figured the total pushed all of them to focus on mathematical communication and multiple models of representation.

The different ways students used the recording sheet offered an excellent assessment opportunity as well. Some students at more beginning

Cerealscapes Recording Sheet

Name __Ella__

__dog__ and __person__ Landscape

I used __69__ plain circles. ◯

I used __26__ colored circles. ◉

I used __10__ squares. ▦

I used __9__ wheels. ▨

I used __0__ other shapes.

Altogether I used __114__ pieces of cereal.

I put mine in tens.

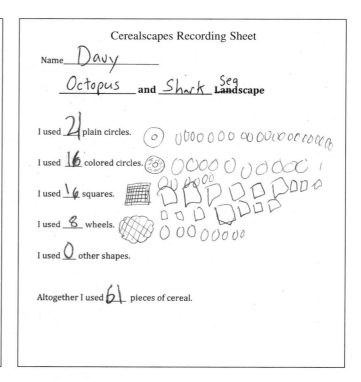

Cerealscapes Recording Sheet

Name __Davy__

__Octopus__ and __Shark__ __Sea__ Landscape

I used __21__ plain circles. ◯

I used __16__ colored circles. ◉

I used __16__ squares. ▦

I used __8__ wheels. ▨

I used __0__ other shapes.

Altogether I used __61__ pieces of cereal.

stages of number-sense development drew every individual piece of cereal on their recording sheets and counted each by ones.

Other students clearly had more comfort connecting the numeric symbols to the quantities and did their addition symbolically.

We also asked students to explain how they figured out the total number of cereal pieces they used for their picture. Some students referred to using tens, and others explained how they added the various numbers on their recording sheet. This small writing sample proved to be illuminating and a very useful assessment of students' basic number concepts.

LESSON

Potato and Apple Stamping

Grade Level: K–2

Math Content Area: Algebra

Math Overview: In this activity students recognize, create, and extend patterns. They use mathematical vocabulary to describe the patterns and make predictions.

Guiding Questions:
Can you make a pattern with your stamps?
What is the pattern? How can you describe it?
Can you predict what shape comes next in your pattern?

Vocabulary: pattern, repeating, predict, square, circle, triangle, rectangle

Materials: potato stamps, apple stamps, adding-machine tape or strips of construction paper, tempera paint

This activity works well as a center or at one table in the classroom. Cover the table and place a few different paint colors in small containers. Slice a potato or turnip in ways that result in different-shaped bases. The cutting needs to be done by an adult because it requires a sharp knife and reasonable eye-hand coordination.

Have students dip a potato stamp in paint and stamp the shapes in a pattern along a strip of paper. Make sure students know not to mix paint colors by dipping the same stamp into more than one paint container. This detail is essential for many art activities and will serve students well in the future.

Once students have made their patterns, ask them to "read" the pattern to a partner or adult at the table. For example, the proceeding pattern reads, "Triangle, triangle, square, triangle, triangle, square . . ."

When students show proficiency in creating and reading their patterns, challenge them to make predictions. Can they tell what shape would come next if the pattern were extended? How far can they go? Another approach involves folding the last part of the strip over on itself. See if students know what shapes are hidden under the fold.

These paper strips can be stapled and turned into decorative headbands. Students can wear their headbands and have friends "read" their patterns.

LESSON

Polygon Fruit Bowl Still Life

Grade Level: K–2

Math Content Areas: Geometry

Math Overview: To create polygon fruit bowl still lifes students need to describe and classify various shapes. They recognize that components of the environment are made up of various shapes. They combine and overlap shapes to make other shapes. They also explore depth and create two-dimensional representations of three-dimensional objects.

Guiding Questions:
What shapes do you see in the fruit bowl?
What are the names and features of the shapes?
How can you combine and overlap shapes to make new shapes and show depth?

Vocabulary: square, triangle, circle, equal, vertex, side, overlap, position, depth

Materials: *Polygon Template* sheet (see appendix and CD), scissors, glue sticks, 9-by-12-inch construction paper, bowl of fruit

Depending on time constraints and the focus of the lesson, teachers can either provide precut construction paper polygons or have students cut their own. Also, students can bring in a fruit from home so that multiple fruit bowls can be created throughout the classroom.

Start the lesson by introducing the idea of a still life and show some examples. (Refer to Chapter 5, "Paper," for more on still lifes.) Then have students focus on the bowl of fruit. Discuss what they see: shapes, colors, lines, shadows, and so on. Record the vocabulary words on the board. Remind students that artists look closely at the world and use different materials to express what they see and feel.

Position the fruit bowl and the students in such a way that everyone can see the bowl. Give students white or black construction paper to use as the background. Then have them use the construction paper polygons to create a rendition of the fruit bowl they see. Having the cutout shapes as tangible models helps students touch and feel the sides and where the lines of the shape meet (vertices). Encourage students to use vocabulary words from the board as they create and discuss their work. Prompt them to notice how they might combine shapes to make new shapes (for example, two triangles can make a square). These observations form a basis for geometric thinking and will also serve students well in some measurement tasks, particularly in finding area.

Encouraging students to find ways to overlap the polygons supports both their math and their art development. By overlapping the shapes, students are deconstructing and recombining polygons to create new shapes. They are also seeing how overlapping shapes, their relative size, and their position on the paper can create an illusion of depth or three dimensions on a two-dimensional plane.

The finished projects look lovely on a bulletin board or posted throughout the classroom. The use of bright construction paper colors with basic geometric shapes gives the pieces a familiar yet striking quality. And the fruit from the bowls makes a tasty fruit salad.

LESSON

Polyhedra Food Sculptures

Grade Level: 2–5

Math Content Area: Geometry

Math Overview: This activity allows students to explore the attributes of polyhedra by constructing them and describing their features. This highly flexible investigation can be adapted to almost any grade; in fact secondary teachers saw potential for its use in their classrooms. As a foundational geometry exploration, polyhedra food sculptures can be revisited throughout the years, building upon previous concepts and vocabulary to expand students' understanding of three-dimensional geometry.

Guiding Questions: What shapes do you see in this polyhedron?

What are the names and features of different polyhedra?

How many faces/edges/vertices does this polyhedron have?

Vocabulary: polyhedron, edge, vertex, vertices, face, flat, base, cube, pyramid, plane, rectangular prism, triangular prism, two-dimensional, three-dimensional

Materials: mini-marshmallows, cheese puffs, or gumdrops (clay can be substituted for the food), toothpicks, *Polyhedra Food Sculptures* recording sheets (see appendix and CD)

This activity connects well with Buckminster Fuller's geodesic domes and other geometric design structures. Sharing some images of his work and telling a bit about his background intrigues students and gives them a real-world context for the structures they create.

We were fortunate to have many different teachers teach this lesson across the grade levels. The activity proved to be adaptable, engaging, challenging, and full of mathematics. The basic structure of the activity remained the same throughout the grade levels.

1. Model how to create polyhedra by connecting toothpicks with marshmallows or gumdrops.
2. Give students some time to practice and explore making their own structures.
3. Provide the *Polyhedra Food Sculptures* recording sheet that directs students to make specific polyhedra. The recording sheet also has students focus on the features of different polyhedra (faces, edges, and vertices).
4. Have students share their creations and discoveries about polyhedra.
5. Challenge upper-grade students to look for relationships between the number of faces, edges, and vertices. See if they can make any conjectures or generalizations based on the data on their recording sheets.

The following descriptions illuminate ways in which the same activity can be adjusted to meet the needs of students at different grade levels. We hope in providing these different variations that teachers will feel encouraged to apply this flexibility in choosing and planning the activities they do with their students.

Polyhedra Food Sculptures with Second Graders

Melissa Ward implemented this activity during math center time in her second-grade classroom. In a brilliant move, she actually copied a worksheet from the second-grade textbook that showed a variety of labeled polyhedra. Melissa saw the opportunity to take a dull workbook page and bring it to life by integrating a hands-on art component. Rather than just passively viewing some two-dimensional pictures of three-dimensional shapes, Melissa's students used the two-dimensional pictures as a jumping-off point to actually create the three-dimensional objects.

Melissa paired students so that they worked together on creating their polyhedra and completing the recording sheet. She guided them in building the cube first. Because it was the simplest and most familiar shape, it posed the fewest challenges, and Melissa was able to focus on connecting the vocabulary to the parts of the cube. She asked students to identify the vertices, edges, and faces of the cube. She also had them explicitly connect the features of the polyhedron to its component parts. Students recognized that the marshmallows were vertices, the toothpicks were edges, and the flat areas between toothpicks on the same plane were the faces.

Once the partners understood the mechanics of building the cube and were clear on the vocabulary, Melissa allowed them to choose other polyhedra to make. They used a recording sheet to keep track of their work. The recording sheet also gave them the further challenge of moving from two-dimensional pictures, to three-dimensional constructions, back to two-dimensional representations of their constructions on the recording sheet.

Melissa noticed that some of her students miscounted the vertices. Sometimes they would skip an edge and its corners, and other times they would count the same feature more than once. This observation prompted her to stop the exploration and have a discussion with the class. She asked them what was tricky about counting the vertices, edges, and faces. She then asked if anyone had found ways to keep track of what they had already counted and what they needed to count. Students shared strategies such as trying to remember where they started, having their partner keep track, double-checking, and marking the starting point so they would know when they had come back around to the beginning. The activity went beyond geometry and also helped students see the need to become more systematic and organized—two very important qualities for mathematicians.

Polyhedra Food Sculptures in a Second-Grade Bilingual Classroom

Priscilla Barcellos led this activity with her second graders in a bilingual classroom, adapting it to accommodate the needs of her English language learners. She called the activity "*Construir Figuras Sólidas*/Constructing Solid Figures." To start the lesson she showed students three figures that she

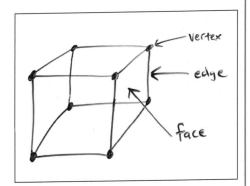

had constructed: a cube, a pyramid, and a rectangular prism. She then told them the lesson objective. "*Yo voy a construir tres figuras sólidas y contar sus caras, aristas, y esquinas.*" (I am going to make three solid figures and count their faces, edges, and corners.) While making each structure she walked around the room and did a think-aloud about how she was making it and what the marshmallows and toothpicks represented. Then she had different students touch different parts to identify vertices, edges, and faces.

She followed up by asking students if they knew the names of the figures, and wrote them on the board. She then used the cube to show them what each part was. She made the connection between the toothpick representing the edge and the marshmallow representing the vertex. She explained that the plane figures on each side of the structure represented the faces.

She had one student from each table group get the materials for their table. She modeled how to make the cube in front of the document camera and had students follow along step-by-step. Some students caught on quickly and went ahead and created theirs on their own. Other students benefited from the detailed modeling that Priscilla provided. As she modeled making the cube, she used a lot of academic vocabulary words such as *edge, vertex, square,* and *plane figure.*

Once all students completed the cube, Priscilla had them grab their cube and put their hands or finger on the part they were counting. For example, she asked them to put their hands on the top face. Then they counted the faces chorally with Priscilla as she moved her flat hand from face to face. They wrote down the number of faces and repeated this with every part of the cube, the pyramid, and the rectangular prism. They used their fingers to trace each edge of the figures. Priscilla also pointed out that the vertices were like corners, where three or more toothpicks met at a marshmallow and the figure changed direction. Connecting the vertex to the idea of a corner is important, because not all marshmallows in the structure were vertices. Some were in the middle of an edge.

After students completed the work on their initial three shapes, they continued to create and explore other polyhedra.

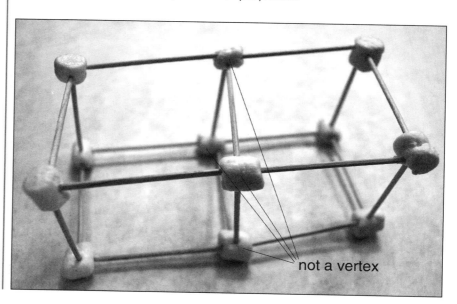

not a vertex

Polyhedra Food Sculptures with Older Students

Alejandra Burt taught the lesson to her fourth graders. It proved interesting to them, and she extended the mathematics to make it worthwhile and rigorous.

To open the lesson and tap prior knowledge, Alejandra drew a square and a cube on the board. She asked students what the two shapes had in common and what some of the differences were. Right away students talked about the cube being three-dimensional. They needed a little guidance when it came to vocabulary such as *faces, vertices*, and *edges*. But once she prompted them, they began to raise their hands.

Then Alejandra introduced the materials that students would be using. She discussed what she wanted them to put on the recording sheet. It was the students' job to construct the polyhedra and count the number of faces, edges, and vertices. She did not give them a lot of instruction when it came to the actual exploration. Alejandra wanted the students to approach the job as a problem-solving activity, so she left it fairly open and let the students find their own ways to count and keep track of their polyhedra attributes. She gave them a good period of time to fill out the recording sheet. She also included two challenge problems. She asked them to look for relationships between the number of faces, edges, and vertices of a polyhedron. She also asked them to describe any discoveries with words or numbers.

Then she put a class chart on the board and had students help her complete it. She gave students some time to discuss and figure out the relationship between the faces, vertices, and edges. They discovered that the number of vertices plus the number of faces is two more than the number of edges. She connected this relationship to mathematical notation, writing, $V + F = E + 2$.

She then told them this mathematical relationship exists in all polyhedra and is called Euler's Formula. Alejandra was pleased that her students did not just learn an equation but actually discovered it for themselves.

Alejandra extended the activity the next day. She used the polyhedra food sculptures to write riddles and modeled one example with the whole class.

My Polyhedra Food Sculpture has twelve edges.
It has eight vertices.

Polyhedron	# Faces	# Vertices	# Edges	
cube	6	8	12	
triangular pyramid	4	5	7	$F + V = E - 2$
rectangular prism	5	6	9	$F + V + 2 = E$
square pyramid	5	5	8	

I used twelve toothpicks to make it.
It has all right angles.

The students guessed that her riddle was about a cube. After they showed their clear understanding of how to write and solve a riddle, Alejandra set them off to work on some more. Pairs of students picked a polyhedron to write a riddle about. After they wrote their riddles, they switched with another pair to try to solve each other's riddles.

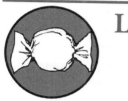

LESSON | Pasta and Pipe-Cleaner Playgrounds

Grade Level: 3–5

Math Content Areas: Number and Operations, Geometry, Measurement

Math Overview: In this activity students use various kinds of pasta and pipe cleaners to create structures for a miniature playground. They engage in geometric processes by visualizing, planning, and building three-dimensional structures. They further their geometric skills by subsequently making two-dimensional drawings of their three-dimensional creations. Students also practice linear measurement through finding and recording the length, width, and height of their structure. Finally, students use estimation and addition to find the total number of pasta pieces in their structure.

Guiding Questions:

Number and Operations
> How many pieces of pasta did you use?
> How many pipe cleaners did you use?
> How many items did everyone at your table use? How many did the whole class use?

Geometry
> How might you bend the pipe cleaners to make different polygons?
> How might you bend and combine pipe cleaners to make different polyhedra?
> How can you combine the materials to help your structure stand up?

Measurement
> About how long/wide/tall is your structure?
> Can you estimate your structure's dimensions in inches or centimeters? How might you do that?

Vocabulary: polygon, polyhedron, two-dimensional, three-dimensional, length, width, height, estimate, inch, centimeter

Materials: pipe cleaners, pasta, *Pasta and Pipe-Cleaner Playgrounds* recording sheets (see appendix and CD), foam board or designated table for finished pieces

We introduced this activity to Sharon Fargason's third graders by asking them if they'd ever been to a playground or park. We continued with a quick partner talk. Each child turned to another child sitting nearby and told what types of things they'd find at a playground or park. They quickly generated a long list that we recorded on chart paper. The list included such items as swings, monkey bars, slides, water fountains, picnic tables, trees, basketball courts, soccer fields, and much more.

Next we gave students the task of making items for a mini-playground. We showed them a piece of 3-by-4-foot foam board and explained that the entire park needed to fit within the board. To further reinforce this idea we asked about how big a person would be if the whole park were the size of the board. We agreed that people would be about the size of a thumb. This informal use of scale helped students keep a semi-consistent standard when working on their pieces. Showing some images of Calder's mobiles and circus sculptures opened students up to the types of images and structures they might design.

We showed the students their materials. They were both surprised and excited to see pasta and pipe cleaners. We gave them a few moments to talk in small groups about what they might make and how they might use the materials. Specifically we asked them to think about how to get their pieces to stand up. We demonstrated how difficult it is to get a piece of pasta or a single straight pipe cleaner to stand on its own. Students generated a lot of good ideas. They suggested folding the pipe cleaners, twisting them together to make square or triangular bases, making spirals, and stringing them through the pasta to make more solid structures. We talked about the stability of triangles and their role as a foundational shape for designing structures. Connecting these ideas to Buckminster Fuller's geodesic dome design helped students conceptualize the construction of complex structures from simple shapes and materials. (In fact the geodesic dome was a popular playground structure in the 1970s.)

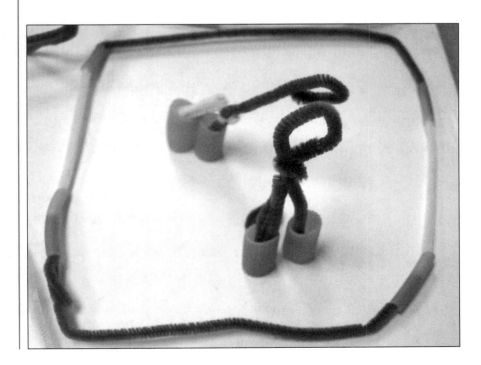

When the students showed they had the necessary ideas to get started, we sent them back to their tables to get to work. Knowing they'd need some time to explore the materials and experiment with different configurations, we allowed them some loose time at the beginning. Then after a little while we had them focus on their playground structure. Students worked quite intently and came up with a variety of solutions to the challenge of creating the structures and getting them to stand up.

After about twenty minutes we brought the students back to the rug to share what they'd done so far. Kevin showed the slide he'd made and talked about how he'd made it. We followed this by estimating the length, width, and height of Kevin's slide in centimeters. We reminded students that a centimeter is about the length of their pinky nail. Then we modeled using a ruler to measure. We also introduced the recording sheets so that as students completed their structures, they'd be ready to move on to the next portion of the job.

Students learned a good deal about structure and design while practicing some important measurement and estimation skills. The structures looked beautiful, and together they made a fantastical playground scene.

LESSON | # Candy Block Sculptures

Grade Level: | 3–5

Math Content Area: | Number and Operations, Geometry, Measurement

Math Overview: | Students use cube-shaped, wrapped candies to create structures. Planning and building these three-dimensional sculptural pieces requires students to address issues of scale, balance, and features of solid structures. Students also explore the need for solid bases in freestanding structures. The candy block structures provide a context for geometrical drawing, measurement, and estimation as students draw and write information about their creations.

Guiding Questions: | **Number and Operations**
About how many candy cubes did you use for your sculpture?
Can you make an estimate without counting every single candy? How?
How many candies did your whole table/group use?

Geometry
What's challenging about drawing your sculpture?
What are some strategies for drawing a three-dimensional object on a flat piece of paper?

Measurement
How can you measure the length, width, and height of your structure?
What tools might you use?
What unit of measurement makes sense to use? Why?

Vocabulary: | length, width, height, estimate, three-dimensional, perspective, centimeter, unit, cube, rectangular prism

Materials: | individual baggies with cube-shaped or rectangular prism–shaped individually wrapped candies (we used Now and Laters, caramels, and Starbursts), rulers, *Candy Block Sculptures* recording sheets (see appendix and CD)

We did this activity with Sharon Fargason's third graders as a follow-up to the *Pasta and Pipe-Cleaner Playgrounds* activity. We told the students that we were so impressed with their playground structures that we wanted to give them a challenge. The activity does not necessarily need to be connected with the *Pasta and Pipe-Cleaner Playgrounds*, but it was a good fit for us.

We showed a "challenge chart." On it we had written several possible structures the students could attempt to create:

- a tall building
- a pyramid
- stair steps
- a bridge
- a wall
- a building with a door

- a building with a window
- a chair
- a desk
- a table

We chose a variety of objects that had varying degrees of challenge, thus differentiating the lesson for students. They could choose to create a sculpture at the appropriate level of challenge for them rather than the teacher demanding the exact same product from everyone.

After we explained the basic activity, we showed the students the materials they needed to use for the sculpture. We held up a baggie containing twenty to thirty mixed wrapped candies. The students expressed extreme enthusiasm and excitement.

Because we were using candy, we knew we had to be very clear about materials management and expectations. We anticipated their questions: Could they keep it? How much could they eat? What if someone had more than someone else? Could they trade candies with someone else for different flavors or types? We answered these questions and reduced the anxiety level to zero by simply telling the students that the candy belonged to their teacher, Ms. Fargason. She would get all the candy back when the lesson ended. She might decide to share some of it later, but that was up to her. This approach made candy distribution, sharing, and collection very easy. Because the candy didn't belong to the students, they didn't worry about who had more or less. They comfortably shared and combined their allotments to create sculptures and didn't consider hoarding or micro-accounting.

Students went back to their tables with their candy bags and set to work on their sculptures.

We circulated and prompted them to explain their plan for creating the desired structure. We also asked them if they thought they had enough candy blocks to achieve their goal. This prompted some estimation and computation: if I'm going to make a house with four walls and each wall

needs nine blocks, how many blocks do I need altogether?

Some students decided to work together and combined their candies to create larger, more detailed pieces. As students completed their work, they raised their hands. We took digital photos of their structures and then gave them copies of the *Candy Block Sculptures* recording sheets and rulers so they could draw and measure their creations.

LESSON | Candy Block Patterns

Grade Level: 3–5

Math Content Area: Algebra

Math Overview: Students use wrapped candy block pieces to create patterns. The patterns may be linear or geometric and are recorded in a variety of ways. These multiple recording methods emphasize the idea that the same data may be represented in a variety of contexts. Students create T-tables to see numeric patterns and make predictions.

Guiding Questions:
What patterns do you notice?
How can we connect these patterns to numbers?
Can you predict what the seventeenth candy in the pattern will be? How do you know?

Vocabulary: pattern, prediction, odd, even, multiple

Materials: a variety of individually wrapped candies, paper, pencil

Artists, architects, and designers employ two- and three-dimensional patterns in their work. Wayne Thiebaud's paintings of rows of cupcakes or slices of pie on a countertop are a visual treat. Patterns are both an aesthetic organizing principle and an important component of structural engineering. Once students become aware of patterns, they begin to detect all types of patterns in the natural and the built environment, from ripples on a pond to a checkerboard. Seeking, recognizing, and describing patterns form the fundamentals of algebraic thinking.

We used the block-shaped candy from the prior activity in Sharon Fargason's class. We challenged students to take the candy from their baggies and create patterns. Most of the students built linear, repeating patterns (red Starburst, caramel, red Starburst, caramel . . .). Students shared some of their patterns with their tablemates. We pushed on the mathematics by asking them to connect their candy patterns to numbers and make predictions. We wrote the following on the board:

R	C	R	C	R	C
1	2	3	4	5	6

We asked students what they noticed. They commented on the numbers getting bigger and going up by one each time. We asked them to look at odd and even numbers to see if they noticed any connections to the pattern. Students quickly realized that the red Starbursts were all odd and the caramels were all even. One student added that the caramels were the numbers you say when you count by twos. We connected this observation to the statement, "The caramels are multiples of two."

We pushed them further by asking if they could make predictions. If we had unlimited candy and continued to build this pattern all the way across the room, could they picture what it would look like? Extending and visualizing patterns serves students in both math and art.

We also asked students to predict which type of candy would be in a given position in the pattern. Would the seventeenth candy be a Starburst or a caramel? How did they know? Could they predict for any given number? These questions help students develop their algebraic thinking through recognizing, communicating, and generalizing about patterns.

LESSON Bean and Seed Mosaics

Grade Level: 3–5

Math Content Area: Number and Operations, Geometry, Measurement

Math Overview: In this activity students explore percents in the context of area. They create mosaic designs and pictures using a given mathematical recipe. Students must consider the overall area they have to work with and ways in which they can incorporate the required shapes into that area. They use geometric thinking to consider the location of shapes on a plane and how they might place the shapes without overlapping.

Guiding Questions:

Number and Operations

How can you estimate the amount of area the other shapes will cover?

Geometry

What are some ways you can arrange the shapes on your background?

Measurement

What is the approximate area of the background?

Vocabulary: percent, circle, triangle, quadrilateral, texture, shape, right triangle, trapezoid, parallelogram, rhombus, scalene triangle, obtuse, isosceles

Materials: 9-by-12-inch tagboard or other fairly sturdy backing material, 1-inch graph paper, a variety of dried beans and seeds (kidney, lima, and mung beans, split and black-eyed peas, sunflower and grass seeds, and so on), pencils, glue, toothpicks or other disposable glue spreaders

This activity yields richly textural mosaics of surprising complexity. Give students a "percent recipe" for their mosaic. For example, tell students their design needs to be 50 percent circles, 25 percent triangles, and 10 percent quadrilaterals. Leave 15–20 percent unspecified for background space to allow more creativity and flexibility.

During the introduction, have students brainstorm different types of triangles and quadrilaterals they might use and create a vocabulary chart on the board with accompanying pictures.

Triangles	Quadrilaterals
right	square
equilateral	rectangle
isosceles	trapezoid
scalene	parallelogram
obtuse	rhombus
acute	

Also discuss how the different areas might be achieved. For example, the 50 percent circle could be one large circle that covers half the tagboard. Or it could be a series of smaller circles that together add up to about 50 percent of the space. Having students explore the options presented by different shapes and relative size allows them to do a lot of computational estimation. It also challenges them to make aesthetic choices. How will they differentiate the shapes from the background? How many shapes will they use? What sizes of beans work best for each shape? Will they use colors and textures to make patterns within the shapes?

Let students sketch their design with pencil on the tagboard.

Emphasize that the shapes will not exactly match the targeted percentages, but that students need to estimate and do mental computation to get close. These sketches require both geometric and number sense and may require several tries before achieving the desired outcome. Encourage students to talk to each other and justify their rationale for choosing the shapes and sizes in their sketches. Some students find it helpful to draw their sketches on 1-inch graph paper. That way, they can more easily estimate the area of the shapes and see if they came close to the targeted percent totals.

When they have a design that meets the criteria, they use glue to cover each shape and affix a type of bean or seed to each area. Using a craft stick or similar tool helps spread the glue in a thin layer over each shape. Students choose a bean or seed not used previously in their mosaic to fill in the background space.

Students might follow up with a short writing assignment in which they describe the process they went through to create their mosaics and how they know they followed the recipe relatively accurately.

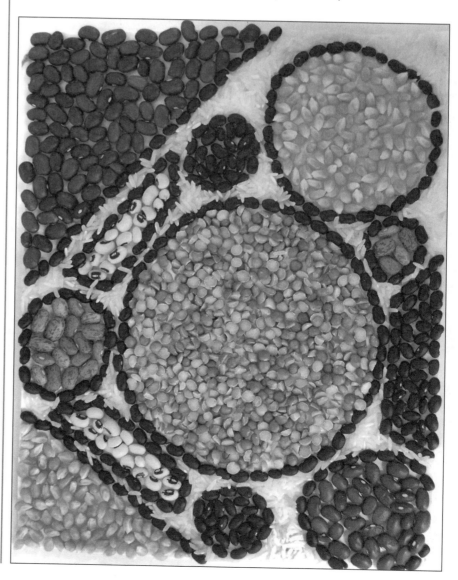

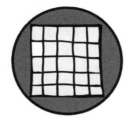

CHAPTER 3

GRIDS AND GRAPH PAPER

Graph paper. It's pretty basic: paper with a bunch of squares on it. If your school site doesn't stock its own supply, an almost infinite variety of graph paper options are easily downloadable. Just search for "graph paper." Not only is graph paper readily available in many sizes, but it is easily modified to create a truly endless variety of squares, rectangles, and arrays. These squares within squares lend themselves to math concepts and activities, and provide a visual, geometric model used by artists throughout history. And then there's a grid, which Dictionary.com defines as "a grating of crossed bars." Thus, graph paper consists of grids.

GRIDS, GRAPHS, AND THE MATHEMATICS

Mathematicians and math students use grids and graph paper for many reasons. Obviously, graph paper can be used for graphing. Coordinate grids, the *x*- and *y*-axes, and ordered pairs all materialize on graph paper. Growth patterns can be displayed and extended via the coordinate graph.

ACTIVITY	GRADES	NUMBER AND OPERATIONS	ALGEBRA	GEOMETRY	MEASUREMENT	DATA ANALYSIS AND PROBABILITY
Tens Art	K–2	✓		✓		
Rectangle Flips	K–2	✓			✓	
Decimal Art	3–5	✓		✓		
Fractions and Decimals	3–5	✓		✓		
Mystery Designs	3–5	✓		✓		
Percent Recipes	3–5	✓		✓		
Decimal Grid Quilt	3–5	✓		✓	✓	
Scaled-Up Pictures	3–5			✓	✓	

Younger children use the grid patterns of five-frames and ten-frames to help them visualize and internalize those early benchmark numbers and the ways in which they can be broken apart and recombined. Numerical values can be ascribed to the squares within a grid so that students can simultaneously view a geometric and numerical model as part of our number system.

The popular hundreds chart is such a labeled ten-by-ten grid. Upper-elementary-grade students use graph paper for a multitude of math tasks. Graph paper offers a model for fractions, decimals, and percents. It also allows older students to undertake ratio and proportion tasks such as scaling up or scaling down. The students can use scaling activities to help them develop visual, geometric models of ratio and proportion ideas. Indeed graph paper's possibilities are immense. It's systematic, organized, and very visual—perfect for math and visual art.

Graph paper is also an important tool in mapping the planes or faces of objects. Students can easily visualize a three-dimensional pyramid when the sides are mapped on two-dimensional graph paper. The conceptual leap from two-dimensional to three-dimensional visualizing and spatial thinking plays an important role in our growth as learners. The ability to translate back and forth from two dimensions to three dimensions is a complex process, but starting early to make these visual connections can assist in the understanding of many important mathematical concepts and processes.

GRIDS, GRAPHS, AND THE ART CONNECTIONS

The grid is a foundational element in all forms of art production. It crosses every culture and time period. From our earliest architectural forms to everyday decorative arts we can see the grid as a basis of design. In fact, the

perfectly proportioned great pyramids of Egypt and the Aztec temples were constructed on a square grid. The marble floors of the Basilica San Marcos in Venice and the intricate tile designs of Islamic art in North Africa and Spain rely on a grid pattern as the basic visual organizing element. Buddhist stupas, mandalas, and Navajo sand paintings are all organized around grids and grid patterns.

The grid also arises in the production of popular arts, commercial art, and decorative arts in everything from patterned wallpapers to comic strips to international historic art styles, such as Art Deco. Contemporary artists Agnes Martin, Carl Andre, and Chuck Close use a formal grid structure in their work. We can see grid patterns in the color theory works of Josef Albers, the quilts of Faith Ringgold, and the enlarged photographic dot paintings of Roy Lichtenstein. Bauhaus, the most influential design school of the twentieth century, reduced almost all design and architecture to the basic grid.

In the 1950s and 1960s artists began to experiment with new approaches to making art. Art started to reflect society's transition into modernist contemporary culture. Artists created works about the rapidly changing cultural environment, their personal explorations in spiritual dimensions, and new scientific discoveries. They pioneered new theories and art movements that significantly changed the art world. Minimalism emerged as an artistic movement that was a redirection from the more personal works of Expressionism. It consciously moved away from personal aesthetic expression toward pure geometric form, often using grids and graph paper as a guide. Josef Albers, Sol LeWitt, and others challenged the traditional notions of art. They deleted all representational imagery and worked exclusively within the formal structures of geometry.

Carl Andre, a sculptor of great influence, helped found Minimalism. In the 1960s he sought to eliminate all that was considered extraneous and decorative from artwork. The result was work that was reduced to basic geometric forms, grids, and minimal color. Precise placement of forms, often cubes or rectangles in a grid pattern, is a signature of his work.

Josef and Anni Albers influenced a generation of artists through their teaching. Initially an elementary school teacher in Germany, Josef met Anni, his wife, at the famous Bauhaus School, where she studied textiles and he worked primarily in glass. Important in the field for blending traditional craft and fine art, they both came to the United States to teach at Black Mountain College in North Carolina in 1933. There Josef initiated a series of paintings based on squares within squares called *Homage to the Square*. He experimented with placing squares of varying hues inside and next to each other with an overall grid. These experiments later developed into his influential color theory. Some student work in this chapter might actually resemble *Homage to the Square*.

Artistic movements continued to evolve with society through the next several decades. The Conceptualism movement paid as much attention to the process as to the product of making art. Considered both a Conceptualist and Minimalist artist, Sol LeWitt made a significant impact on the historic transformation of contemporary art in the 1960s. LeWitt worked in many mediums, in both two and three dimensions, but is most known for his large Minimalist "wall drawings." The artwork consisted of a set of instructions to a gallery or museum to create a drawing directly on the wall. These engaging, visually simple, and powerful line drawings signified process and spatial experience. They also challenged viewers to think about what it means to employ nonartists to make art. LeWitt continued to make artwork and challenge aesthetic ideas until his death in 2007. Members of the art world consider him an American icon and one of the most important artists of the twentieth century.

As has happened with many artists, Piet Mondrian and Agnes Martin's spiritual studies influenced their work. Although they lived and worked in different countries and time periods, both used the grid as a formal element and subject matter in their paintings. Born in 1872 in the Netherlands, Piet Mondrian practiced painting while teaching elementary school early in his career. He studied Theosophy, a spiritual movement that was popular in the late nineteenth century and continued to influence his work throughout his life. He later moved to Paris, then London, then New York, where he produced many of his most recognizable works in the abstract style of painting grids and rectangles in primary colors.

Agnes Martin was famous for her subtle monochromatic paintings. Born in Canada in 1912, she pursued a life of solitude and spiritual investigation through her art. Many of her paintings and drawings, which she considered Abstract Expressionistic, consisted only of grids or lines. She was highly regarded in the contemporary art world even though she rarely exhibited her work. She lived for fifty years in Taos, New Mexico.

An underlying grid pattern is visible in the work of artists whose work is as different as that of Faith Ringgold and Chuck Close. Faith Ringgold is well known for what she terms "painted story quilts." These large painted and sewn fabric wall hangings often examine issues of racism and sexism through narratives from her life growing up in Harlem. The grid determines the formal structure and pattern in all quilts. Ringgold has written and illustrated many children's books. *Tar Beach* was a Caldecott Honor Book and winner of the Coretta Scott King Award for Illustration.

Chuck Close is famous for his greatly enlarged close-up portraits of people's faces. He works in a variety of media: drawing, painting, photography, and printmaking. He employs the grid to scale up his images without altering the proportions. Using a grid to scale up images is an important technique artists have used for centuries. Often intentionally leaving the grid exposed in the final work, Close chooses to reveal and highlight his process and the role of the grid in creating art.

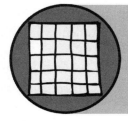

Grids and Graphs Art Vocabulary: Abstract, Abstract Expressionism, aesthetic, Art Deco, asymmetry, Conceptualism, hue, medium, Minimalism, monochromatic, portraits, primary colors, proportion, sculpture, symmetry

THE GRIDS AND GRAPHS LESSONS

Let's take a look at where grids and graph paper intersect in the math and visual arts worlds. If the goal is to teach math through visual art, what can be done with graph paper? A lot. How did fifth graders create such masterpieces as *Strawberries and Lemons* while practicing computation with decimals? Simple: they used graph paper.

Going into classrooms armed with graph paper and colored pencils, we found many opportunities to engage students. Meaningful math lay at the core of the activities, but the art focus brought the math to light and to life. Following are some examples of grids and graph paper activities at different grade levels.

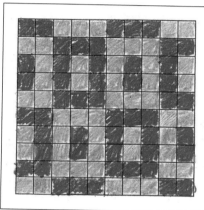

Title: Strawberries and Lemons

Decimal Information:

green: 0.50
pink: 0.50   0.50 + 0.50 = 1
              1.0 - 0.50 = 0.50

LESSON

Tens Art

Grade Level: K–2

Math Content Area: Number and Operations, Geometry

Math Overview: This activity allows young students to manipulate a geometric model of ten. By familiarizing themselves with different configurations and combinations that make ten, students develop a foundational understanding of the key component of the base ten number system.

Guiding Questions:

Number and Operations
How did you make ten?
Can you say and write the equation?
Geometry
What shapes do you see?
Are any shapes the same?
What happens when you rotate your picture?

Vocabulary: addition, equals, tens, benchmark numbers, symmetrical, asymmetrical

Materials: *Ten-by-Ten Grid* and *Hundreds Chart Grid* (see appendix and CD), colored pencils

Students each get a ten-by-ten grid. (This activity can be done with a two-by-five grid for early primary students, who can practice their combinations of 10 rather than 100.) They choose three or four different-colored crayons or pencils. Each color is used to color ten squares at a time on their grid. Each ten squares of the same color need to share at least one side so that they form a connected shape or area. Encourage students to decide in advance if they want to make a symmetrical or asymmetrical design. Have them think and plan in advance to help develop their visual and spatial reasoning abilities. Modeling an example in front of the class helps tremendously.

Students go back and count the total number of squares for each color and the total number of squares. The activity provides an excellent assessment opportunity of basic number concepts. Do the students count by tens or by ones? Are they organized and efficient in their counting methods? Do they recognize the efficiency of using benchmark numbers to navigate our base ten number system? Can they combine groups of ten and count by tens? After processing the mathematics, the grids can be displayed as a quilt or border.

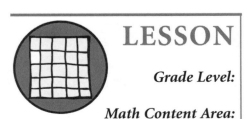

LESSON   Rectangle Flips

Grade Level: K–2

Math Content Area: Number and Operations, Measurement

Math Overview: *Rectangle Flips* give students practice with representing whole numbers in a variety of ways. They take apart and recombine quantities to experience the commutative property of addition. They also connect the area model to whole number arrays, which helps them think flexibly about ways numbers and quantities can be represented.

Guiding Questions:

Number and Operations

How many squares did you color altogether?

Can you make a number sentence that describes what you did?

Measurement

What is the area of your grid? How do you know?

Vocabulary: addition, sum, commutative property, associative property

Materials: different-sized grids (e.g., two-by-five, three-by-four, five-by-ten; *Grids A and B* [see appendix and CD]), crayons or colored pencils

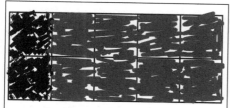

2 + 8 = 10

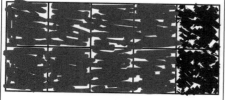

8 + 2 = 10

Assign a specific dimension grid to each student. Choosing different-sized grids based on students' needs allows for differentiated instruction within the same activity. For example, students who need practice with combinations of ten can use a two-by-five grid. Students ready to explore larger numbers can use three-by-four or five-by-five. Have students count the number of squares in their assigned grid. Connect the number of squares to the concept of area.

Have students choose two different colors and create several different designs on their arrays by coloring in all the squares within the grids. Have them connect addition equations to the arrays they generated. This activity can also be helpful in visualizing the commutative property. Have students choose one of their colored grids and rotate it or flip it upside down. Then they rewrite the addition equation based on the new order of the colors they see.

Help them see that although the designs and equations look different, the addends are the same (commutativity). Repeat the activity with three or more colors to offer a visual model of the associative property.

LESSON # Decimal Art

Grade Level: 3–5

Math Content Areas: Number and Operations, Geometry

Math Overview: *Decimal Art* provides students with models for addressing place value and decimal numbers. By connecting fractions to decimal numbers students use familiar fraction benchmarks to generate decimal representations. Using a ten-by-ten grid reinforces the structure of the base ten system and gives students a bridge between visual models and symbolic notation.

Guiding Questions:

Number and Operations

How are fractions and decimals the same?

How are they different?

Geometry

Why is a ten-by-ten grid useful when you're working on decimals?

Vocabulary: grid, decimal, fraction, percent, pattern, design

Materials: pencils, *Decimal Chart Grid* (see appendix and CD), two-color grid samples, colored pencils

We used grids for several lessons in Tina Rasori's fifth-grade classroom to help students visualize the connection between decimals, fractions, and percents. The grids also helped students add and subtract with decimals. First we showed them some grid pieces that we created. We deliberately scaffolded the viewing so that the first image was obviously half of the square.

By showing this simple image first we hoped to give access to all the students. Even if they were not comfortable with the symbolic notation, they could at least name the shaded area as "one-half" and then we could model writing the symbol. Students named the shaded area as a fraction, a decimal, and a percent. We modeled writing the names.

From there we moved on to increasingly challenging images. We presented an image and then had students talk to a partner about the shaded portion and how to name it as a fraction, decimal, and/or percent.

Then students were given the task of creating their own pattern, design, or pictures on decimal grids. The task entailed labeling the shaded portion as a fraction, decimal, and percent. For this introductory activity we made the rule that students had to color in whole squares only. They couldn't use curved lines or parts of a small square. This rule both simplified the activity and kept the focus on "parts of one hundred"—a mathematically crucial concept for percents and for helping students understand the decimal system's connection to our base ten number system.

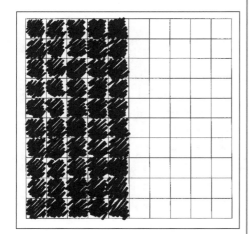

The students succeeded with this activity both mathematically and artistically. They diligently worked on their decimal art and eagerly shared their creations with their tablemates. They accurately labeled their work, occasionally struggling to count all the shaded squares in the more complicated designs.

We concluded the session by having students share their work and talk about what they had learned from the experience. Many of them expressed enthusiasm for the opportunity to be creative and do art. Several of them liked the fact that they got to use art to help them do math. Some commented on their ability to see the decimals on their papers. Tina sent blank decimal grids home, and students continued to create and label their pieces for further practice. These homework grid designs brightened up part of a wall in the classroom.

The next session we moved on to adding and subtracting decimal numbers. We began by showing some examples of grids and tiling activities done by several artists: *Grid Mounted* and *Homage to the Square* by Josef Albers, and *Broadway Boogie Woogie* by Piet Mondrian. Next we showed

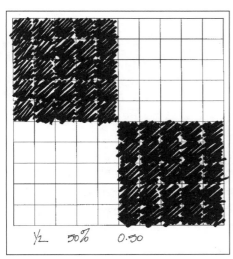

½   50%   0.50

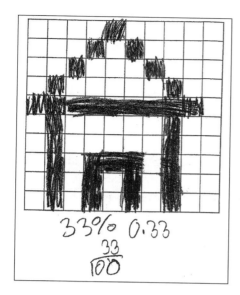

33% 0.33 $\frac{33}{100}$

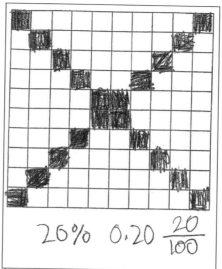

20% 0.20 $\frac{20}{100}$

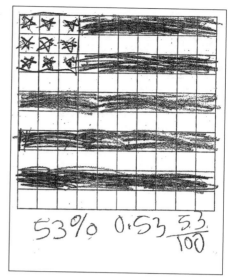

53% 0.53 $\frac{53}{100}$

the students a few sample designs we had created using two different-colored pencils and had them describe the addition equation that corresponded to the visual images.

We showed a few more examples, each time pushing the mathematics a bit further. The students named the decimal portion of each grid colored. Then we encouraged them to generate both addition and subtraction equations that correlated with the images they viewed. We recorded those equations below the samples.

After we felt confident that students understood the task, they set off to create their own two-color masterpieces. Their enthusiasm was palpable as the opportunity to use colored pencils and the chance to be creative motivated them. Students worked diligently on their creations and recorded the corresponding decimal number equations. The results were both beautiful and mathematically challenging.

To culminate the decimal grid sequence we showed Piet Mondrian's *Lozenge Composition with Yellow, Black, Blue, Red, and Gray*. This grid painting is oriented diagonally so the square looks like a diamond. There are large areas of color in the painting, so students could tap in to both their estimation skills and their prior experiences with their own grids to make reasonable estimates about how much of each color Mondrian used.

BLUE 0.50
YELLOW 0.50
0.50 + 0.50 = 1
1 − 0.50 = 0.5

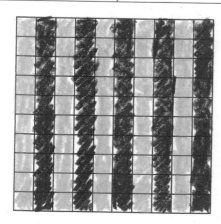

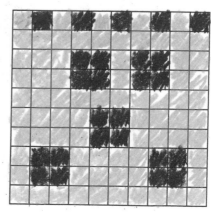

Blue 0.25
Yellow 0.75
0.75 + 0.25 = 1
1 − 0.25 = .75
1 − 0.75 = .25

LESSON | # Fractions and Decimals

Grade Level: | 3–5

Math Content Areas: | Number and Operations, Geometry

Math Overview: | Using fractions to introduce decimals, this activity supports students as they discover equivalent representations of the same number. Students use grids as benchmarks to estimate fractions and connect these fractions to their decimal equivalents.

Guiding Questions: | **Number and Operations**
   Did you color more or less than half?
   About what decimal number describes what you colored?
   Can you make an equation that describes your grid design?
Geometry
   What is the connection between the grid you colored and the addition
      equation you wrote?

Vocabulary: | fraction, decimal, numerator, denominator

Materials: | graph paper, colored pencils, whiteboards (optional)

Sandra Leu modified the *Decimal Art* activity to meet the needs of her third graders.

How did you sequence the activity?
The lesson sequence was much like the lesson I was able to observe with Caren and Lynn. Students first began by generating [a list of] where they have seen fractions or decimals in the world around them to spark prior knowledge. Then we reviewed our knowledge from the previous day about place value and decimal relation with fractions. Then we went over a couple of examples I generated. I asked students to respond using their whiteboards so I could tell who needed more practice and who was ready for independent work.

  Still on the carpet, they worked in partners to generate some student examples on graph paper. They created a picture or pattern on the graph paper and wrote the decimal and fraction relating to the colors of their piece. The others gave students a silent signal of thumbs up or down to indicate whether they agreed or disagreed with their work. Students then had independent time to explore either in partners or by themselves. At the end we did a gallery walk and posted our work around the room with pretend roped-off areas.

How did it go?
The overall activity went well, and the students were able to enjoy the art and math connection. It prompted students to ask if we could integrate more

art into mathematics. Students were excited to have a creative response to mathematics. The roped-off gallery walk ensured that students wanted to try their best and display their best work.

One student created initials of her name. That image led to a lot of student interest. She did struggle a bit with connecting the decimals to the fraction format because she had not previously worked with such large fractions. It helped when students understood the connection between counting the squares of each color and the numerator.

Another student related his love of drawing comics to the fraction activity. He was able to draw a favorite character using the squares. It was refreshing to watch a student who usually struggles with math excel and desire to keep on working.

What did the students learn?

Students strengthened their knowledge of connecting fractions with decimals through a visual example. It also helped a lot of students who were struggling with large fractions and the place value of decimals. I could tell when students who learn visually were able to count the squares and see the larger pattern.

LESSON

Mystery Designs

Grade Level: 3–5

Math Content Area: Number and Operations, Geometry

Math Content Area: Mystery Designs connect to the previous exploratory decimal grid activities and push students to begin using operations on decimal numbers. Students use benchmark grid patterns to determine decimal addends for addition and subtraction equations. They connect the symbolic decimal representations with their geometric counterparts.

Guiding Questions:

Number and Operations

What are different ways to get a sum of 1 with two decimal numbers?
How do those equations connect to fractions?

Geometry

How can you match an equation to a grid design?

Vocabulary: equations, estimations

Materials: grid designs created in *Decimal Art* activity with equations covered, equations written on separate pieces of paper

Use the grid artwork created by students in the previous activities. Students need to match each mystery design with its corresponding equation. For example we showed the class two student-created images, *The Hourglass* and *The Mystery*.

Title: hour glass

Title The Mystery

Then we wrote some equations on the board and asked students to match the equation with its image:

$$0.60 + 0.40 = 1$$
$$1 - 0.49 = 0.51$$
$$0.40 = 1 - 0.60$$

We had the students talk in pairs for a few moments and then asked individuals to explain their answers and the thinking behind them. These challenging discussions entailed both mathematical and visual arts concepts and vocabulary.

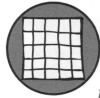

LESSON | # Percent Recipes

Grade Level: | 3–5

Math Content Area: | Number and Operations, Geometry

Math Overview: | Similar to *Mystery Designs*, students develop strategies for recognizing and computing percent numbers. The open-ended nature of the tasks allows students to generate multiple representations of commonly used percents.

Guiding Questions: | **Number and Operations**
How can you tell if something is more than 50 percent or less than 50 percent?
What does 25 percent look like?

If you know what 75 percent looks like, can that help you estimate other percentages? How?

Geometry

If the grid is 100 percent, what percent best describes the color _____?
Can you use the grid to show how you figured it out?

Vocabulary: equation, percent, benchmark, addition, subtraction, commutative property

Materials: *Ten-by-Ten Grids* (see appendix and CD), colored pencils or crayons

Give students a ten-by-ten grid and a "color recipe." For example, the recipe might be 60 percent yellow, 30 percent green, and 10 percent black.

Students use the recipe to create an original design, pattern, or picture that follows the given percentages. Share the pieces and discuss the different effects that result even though the colors stay the same. Ask students how using benchmark numbers (tens) helped them in creating and estimating. Also, the commutative property arises from the different configurations of the same number. Students then create their own recipes and grid art pieces.

After students create a variety of pieces, a *Mystery Design* type of activity can also be used to have students guess which piece fits which recipe. Again, an opportunity for estimating and justifying reasonableness emerges from this investigation. Students can also use this activity to practice generating addition and subtraction equations. For example, 60% + 30% + 10% = 100% or 100% - (60% + 10%) = 30%.

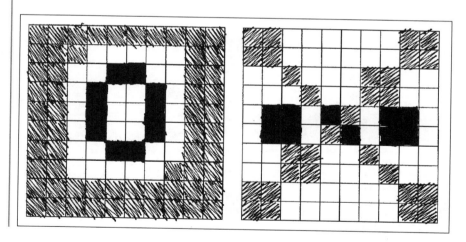

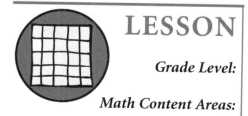

LESSON Decimal Grid Quilt

Grade Level: 3–5

Math Content Areas: Number and Operations, Geometry, Measurement

Math Overview: In *Decimal Grid Quilts* students investigate the results of subdividing and combining two-dimensional shapes. Students represent the shapes they create both as decimal numbers and as area of a square.

Guiding Questions:

Number and Operations

Understand the place-value structure of the base ten number systems and be able to represent and compare whole numbers and decimals.

Geometry

What shapes do you see within the grid?

Can you see shapes in your grid that can be broken down into other shapes?

Can you picture what your grid will look like if you rotate it 90 degrees?

Measurement

What is the area of your grid?

What percent of the area is each color on your grid?

What is the perimeter of your grid? How do you know?

Vocabulary: decimal, area, curved

Materials: *Ten-by-Ten Grids* (see appendix and CD), colored pencils or crayons

This activity is similar to *Percent Recipes* except the students receive decimal numbers to work with. For example, tell the students to color their grid so that 0.50 is blue, 0.25 is yellow, and 0.25 is black. After individuals complete their task, use a bulletin board or a large piece of butcher paper to post all the grids into a quilt.

This *Decimal Grid Quilt* activity can be used with whole numbers and a measurement focus. Students can color ten grids with two or three different colors. They then need to find the area covered by each color. As a challenge students can use curved lines and/or color parts of squares in their pieces. Then they need to estimate the area covered by the irregularly shaped colors. An emphasis on justification and multiple approaches to solving the estimating area problems bring the mathematical reasoning and communication to the forefront.

LESSON | Scaled-Up Pictures

Grade Level: 3–5

Math Content Areas: Geometry, Measurement

Math Overview: This challenging activity prompts students to assess locations and place points and shapes along a coordinate grid. Students also explore the concept of similarity while using measurement skills and strategies to generate accurate representations of two-dimensional designs.

Guiding Questions:

Geometry

How does the coordinate grid system help you locate different parts of the grid?

How can you tell if the new picture is similar to the original picture?

Measurement

How can you find the area of this grid?

What will the area of the new grid be? How do you know?

Vocabulary: grid, vertical, horizontal, diagonal, scale

Materials: postcard or picture divided into coordinate grid pieces; larger similar coordinate grid on piece of butcher paper; paper squares that fit in larger grid; pencils; rulers; colored pencils, crayons, or oil pastels

Use a postcard, a picture from a magazine, or, ideally, a reproduction of a culturally or historically significant artwork. Overlay a grid and cut the picture into equal-sized squares. It will help to start with a fairly large image so that each square will be at least one inch. Number and label the back of each piece with the corresponding number and letter from the grid and an arrow so you know where it belongs and how to orient it on the grid.

Give each student one small square from the deconstructed picture and have the student draw that piece on a larger blank square.

Tell students to copy the number, letter, and arrow of their piece on the back of the larger square first. There are some visual tricks that will help the students to more accurately transfer and scale up each square. Some designs can be very complex, so it always helps to model the process first and have the students practice on a simple image. The secret is to really look at the square, make some mental comparisons, and decide how the lines and shapes are placed. Does a line go from one corner through the middle to halfway up the opposite side? How far apart are the shapes? It can help to measure or imagine where the center point is on each square, lightly draw marks along the sides for corresponding measurements, or draw a full grid to scale on each square.

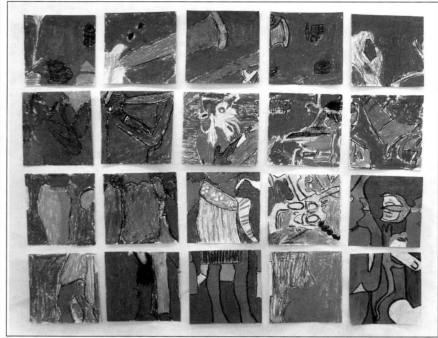

After they have transferred designs, have students put all the enlarged squares back together in their proper places to create a scaled-up (and quite funky-looking) version of the original picture.

It is useful to have rulers for this project, and it's important to have everyone use the same materials and color palette. This allows students to use size, shape, color, and location to match up the squares.

CHAPTER 4

THE ROCK

I t's hard to avoid rocks. They're pretty much everywhere. They come in a variety of sizes, shapes, and colors. They're old, and they tell the stories of our planet and beyond. Kids know a lot about rocks. They collect them, climb them, put them in their pockets, skip them on water, and throw them as far as they can.

We're lumping some clay into this chapter as well. Some activities use both rocks and clay, but most use either one or the other as the primary material. We have found ways to use rocks for building, counting, patterning, and much more. Students' familiarity with rocks and their comfort in manipulating them allowed us to engage them in many ways.

Rocks and pebbles exist in abundance on our planet, but harvesting them is not always convenient. Although you might ask students to bring in some rocks and pebbles, seasonal and regional variations might make it difficult. Fortunately, rocks also abound in the retail world. Consider stocking up at craft stores, pet stores, home and garden shops, rock and masonry building-supply stores, kitchen and bathroom countertop fabrication places, or tile outlets.

ACTIVITY	GRADES	NUMBER AND OPERATIONS	ALGEBRA	GEOMETRY	MEASUREMENT	DATA ANALYSIS AND PROBABILITY
Pebble Clusters	K–2	✓		✓		
Rock Comparing	K–2		✓			
Rock Sorting	K–2		✓			✓
Rock Gardens	K–2	✓		✓		
The *Bear*	K–2, 3–5				✓	
Rock Walls and Forms	K–2, 3–5	✓			✓	
Cave Paintings	K–2, 3–5	✓				
Aquarium Rock Mosaic	3–5	✓		✓	✓	
Stone Buildings	K–2, 3–5			✓	✓	

THE ROCK AND THE MATHEMATICS

Rocks may very well be the ultimate manipulative—cheap, abundant, durable, and available in many sizes, shapes, and colors. These attributes make them excellent for all types of math investigations. Students can sort and classify rocks, compare and order rocks, or weigh and measure them. Rocks make excellent counting and grouping tools as well. The math activities presented in this chapter use rocks and clay both as a context for exploring mathematical ideas and as the medium through which mathematical ideas are expressed.

THE ROCK AND THE ART CONNECTIONS

Rock has always been an important material in the realm of the artist. The earliest man-made sculptures consisted of votive figures made of carved rock. Rock is one of Earth's most durable and abundant materials. Artists value stone not only for its variety and beauty, but also for its strength, density, and capacity for holding fine detail. It also possesses the metaphoric qualities of immortality and permanence. Stonehenge, the Great Wall of China, the Acropolis, and the pyramids in Egypt and Latin America are some of the best-known structures from human history, each made of stone. From the giant carved figures on Easter Island in the South Pacific to Teotihuacan, the largest city in the ancient Americas, stone has long offered both a construction material and a substance with which to express the mysteries of human culture.

People have used stone to create structures, tools, furniture, grave markers, mosaics, and art in every period of human history. Archeologists have found petroglyphs that date from around 29,000 BC. Museums preserve carved rock figures from as far back as 25,000 BC. The famous cave paintings in Lascaux, France, date between 17,000 and 15,000 BC. Michelangelo carved *David* from marble more than 500 years ago, and the sculpture continues to engage and awe audiences today.

Natural rock formations have served as inspiration to artists from many cultures. Contemplative and spiritual images have been carved into rock walls by people in every region of the world. Rock gardens feature significantly in Japanese and Chinese temples. Rocks and rock gardens also turn up frequently in contemporary public spaces.

Rocks have been valued and traded throughout human history. Artists and nonartists alike seem to have a special relationship to rocks. How many of us have had rock collections? Think about how natural it is for a child to carry around a stone or how much value we place on a tiny rock that is worn on a finger. Artists have the opportunity today to explore the newest technologies and materials, but many continue to be drawn to rock, the oldest material of all.

Constantin Brancusi (1876–1957) was a renowned pioneer of modern abstract sculpture. Born in Romania, he lived most of his life in France, and his inspirations came from African images and forms. Although he used traditional sculptural materials such as metal, wood, and stone, he used them to create modernist pieces. One of his most famous pieces, *Bird in Space*, is made of marble. Brancusi's *Bird in Space* revolutionized sculpture by taking a complex subject and reducing it to basic, smooth, rounded elements.

Isamu Noguchi was born in Los Angeles in 1904 to an American mother and a Japanese father. His childhood spent in Japan and the United States greatly influenced his art. In the late 1920s he studied art in Paris and worked in Brancusi's studio. Noguchi learned a great deal about the geometric features of sculpture during this time. He wrote of those years, "Brancusi got me started with carving a flat plane in limestone preparatory to making a base. First he taught me how to correctly cut and true the edges and then by cutting grooves, to level the space between, then on to squaring the cube" (Ashton 1992, 22). Noguchi worked with many materials. He created sculpture, gardens, furniture, lighting fixtures, and set designs for theater and dance. He continued working in the ancient medium of stone when much of the art world was beginning to embrace new technologies, Performance Art, and Pop Art. Whatever materials he used, his uncomplicated aesthetic revealed its physical and metaphoric qualities, a balance of form that resonates with nature and architecture. Museums and public spaces worldwide feature his elegant stone sculptures and contemplative environments. The Noguchi Museum in the borough of Queens, in New York, is dedicated to his work.

Tim Hawkinson creates humorous and awe-inspiring art. He uses everyday materials and seemingly simple techniques to build ingenious sculptural objects. He has created mechanized robots, a "family tree" of craft sticks and pencils, and a 180-ton teddy bear made of rocks. His playful approach to changes in scale and materials poses questions about how we perceive the materials around us and what we know about the physical world. He placed his sculpture *Bear*, 23 feet tall and composed of giant boulders, in a courtyard at the University of California–San Diego between the engineering and technology buildings. The giant but cuddly-looking *Bear*, delightful and simple in appearance, represents an engineering feat that suggests a review of our assumptions about modern technologies and intentions.

Maya Lin's work bridges public art, architecture, landscape, and sculpture. While still an undergraduate student in architecture, Lin was commissioned to design the now famous Vietnam Veterans Memorial wall in Washington, D.C. Lin inscribed this 246-foot-long black granite memorial with the names of the Americans who died during the Vietnam War. The wall stands as a powerful and iconic part of the public landscape.

Lin used stone and water for her Civil Rights Memorial in Montgomery, Alabama, and at Yale University in a tablelike fountain inscribed with numbers that correlate to women enrolled there throughout the years. In her book *Boundaries* she writes of her sculpture titled *Sounding Stones 1 2 3 4*, at the Federal Courthouse Plaza in New York City. She explains using her intention of "turning a fountain inside out" and "turning one's focus inside a work of art" (Lin 2000, 6:24). Her middle name, Ying, means "precious stone."

In the 1970s, Robert Smithson started "Land Art" or "Earthwork," a genre that involves using the landscape and natural materials to create large-scale work. These huge pieces reside in sparsely populated areas away from large cities. Smithson sought to take art out of the galleries and place it in unique natural contexts. His work includes many temporary pieces made of materials found on the site. Smithson created *Spiral Jetty* in Utah. This permanent piece consists of stone, earth, and salt and resides along and partly within the Great Salt Lake.

Rock Art Vocabulary: asymmetry, balance, concentric, contour line, Land Art, landscape, mosaic, pattern, perspective, petroglyph, pictograph, proportion, scale, seascape, shape, symbol, symmetry, texture, three-dimensional, two-dimensional

THE ROCK LESSONS

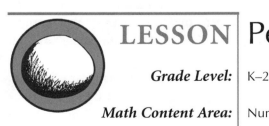

LESSON	# Pebble Clusters
Grade Level:	K–2
Math Content Area:	Number and Operations, Geometry
Math Overview:	*Pebble Clusters* offer an engaging way for students to count, group, and add numbers. By providing visual representations of numbers, students begin to

internalize numerals and the quantities they represent. Through repeated experience with this activity they also develop their ability to subitize, or recognize familiar geometric clusters and their quantities (the way they recognize the numbers on dice without having to count all the dots).

Guiding Questions:

Number and Operations

How many pebbles do you see? How do you know?

Did you group some pebbles together to make it easier to count?

Geometry

How did you look at your pebble cluster?

Did you notice any shapes that helped you count?

Vocabulary: count, group, add, total

Materials: pebbles (ten to twenty), an overhead projector or document camera

This simple activity works throughout the school year and helps students develop their beginning number concepts and number sense.

Start with a small number of pebbles (five to ten) and scatter them on the overhead projector while the projector is turned off. Then turn on the projector and give students a few seconds to figure out the total number of pebbles. Students may attempt to count the pebbles one by one at first. Encourage them to find ways to count and group the pebbles. Over time students will develop more sophisticated ways to group and combine the pebble clusters. For example, students might see the configuration below as 3 + 3 + 3 + 1, or they might see it as 5 + 3 + 2.

Asking students to explain and illustrate their strategies for finding the total number of pebbles helps develop their mathematical communication skills while giving other students the chance to learn different approaches. Students can draw the cluster and circle the way they visualized and grouped the pebbles. Have them write the corresponding equation below the illustration. The visual representations of the pebble clusters make interesting art pieces and can be bound into *Pebble Clusters* books.

Pebble Clusters work well as a homework assignment too. Parents and students can work together to scatter a fistful of pebbles and then try to find the total number in different ways.

$3 + 3 + 3 + 1 = 10$

$5 + 3 + 2 = 10$

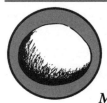

LESSON

Rock Comparing

Grade Level: K–2

Math Content Area: Algebra

Math Overview: *Rock Comparing* gives students experience with identifying and describing attributes. They consider such mathematical features as size, shape, and weight. Using descriptive and mathematical language develops students' abilities to communicate mathematically.

Guiding Questions: What's the same about these rocks?
How are these rocks different?

Vocabulary: same, different, sort, color, size, shape, texture, smooth, jagged

Materials: rocks

Similar versions of the following two activities are described in Chapter 6, "The Shoe." Comparing, sorting, and classifying help young students develop their algebraic thinking. Repeated experiences with a variety of objects assist students in strengthening their conceptual understanding while expanding their vocabulary and flexibility.

Have students sit on the rug in a circle or in some other configuration that allows for easy viewing of a set of objects. Take six to ten assorted rocks and have students notice and describe their different characteristics. Students may remark on color, texture, size, weight, or other attributes. Have them identify ways some rocks are the same and different. Pick two rocks to use as an example. Provide sentence frames: "These rocks are the same because they both have _____."

"These rocks are different because one _____ and the other _____."

Partners can then go back to their seats with two rocks to compare. They can discuss the similarities and differences and record their ideas on a T-table. Many of the descriptive terms students will use to describe the rocks are taken from both math and art vocabulary.

LESSON

Rock Sorting

Grade Level: K–2

Math Content Area: Algebra, Data Analysis and Probability

Math Overview: *Rock Sorting* allows students to group and classify rocks based on different attributes. This activity lays the groundwork for later algebraic thinking by having students seek patterns and consider and describe features and relationships.

Guiding Questions: Can we use a graph to sort the rocks?
How did you group your rocks?
What is your rule for these rocks?
Which rocks don't fit the rule? Where do they go?

Vocabulary: same, different, Venn diagram, circle, texture, shape, color, surface

Materials: rocks, Venn diagram on butcher paper or Hula-Hoops

This activity builds on the *Rock Comparing* experience. Have students sit in a circle on the rug. Put eight to ten assorted rocks in the middle of the circle. Tell the students you are thinking of a secret rule and are going to show them which rocks fit the rule and which rocks don't. Their job is to guess the rule. You might start with a simple rule such as "smooth surface." As you sort the rocks, say to the students, "This rock fits my secret rule" and put it within the circle on the butcher paper or, "This rock doesn't fit my rule" as you move the rock onto the butcher paper outside the circle.

Encourage students to continue to use the vocabulary they learned in the *Rock Comparing* activity. Let them try to guess your secret rule. If they are ready, they can generate their own rules, sort the rocks, and have the class try to guess their rules. Extend this activity by sorting rocks with a two-variable Venn diagram. Simply add another large overlapping circle to your butcher paper. Each circle represents a rule (for example, it has a smooth surface, it has gray in it), and rocks that fit both rules go in the middle of the two circles. The skills of observing, classifying, and considering multiple attributes serve students in art and science as well as math.

LESSON | Rock Gardens

Grade Level: K–2

Math Content Area: Number and Operations, Geometry

Math Overview: This rich art experience gives students ways to count, group, and add objects. Through exploring sets of rocks, students use estimation and mental computation and apply them to addition.

Guiding Questions: **Number and Operations**
About how many rocks did you use in your garden?
Can you estimate how many rocks you used?
How does your estimate compare with the actual amount?
Geometry
How can you place your rocks to create a balance in your garden?
What types of lines will you use to connect your rocks?

Vocabulary: line, curve, spiral, concentric circles, symmetrical, asymmetrical, intersecting, parallel, radial, balance, irregular, pattern, bird's-eye view, estimate, actual, difference, total

Materials:

Rock Garden recording sheet and *Rock Garden Template* (see appendix and CD), black construction paper, glue sticks, 9-by-12-inch white construction paper, pencils, pebbles, rock garden images

We tried this activity in two different second-grade classrooms. Frannie MacKenzie and Lila Murphy both graciously offered their classrooms and students to us. We began the lesson by showing students images of rock gardens (a sample is included on the CD that accompanies the book).

The students had many responses.

"They come from China."
"No, Japan."
"It looks like water."
"It looks like crop circles."
"Maybe a plow made the lines."
"Or maybe a rake."
"Or maybe they're tire tracks."
"I think they're made with special tools."
"It looks like a bird's-eye view."
"It looks like a whirlpool."
"Or a tornado."

After the initial flurry of observations and speculations we asked them to describe specific things they saw and began a rock garden word bank. We helped students connect some of their ideas to the proper vocabulary. The list included words such as *line, curve, balance, odd, even, parallel, asymmetrical,* and *concentric.*

We discussed the visual spatial qualities of the gardens and how the rocks were placed. Japanese temple rock gardens are designed to be contemplative spaces and to represent abstract versions of a landscape or seascape. In these gardens rocks represent islands, mountains, or boats, and the raked sand represents ripples on water. We noticed that there was an asymmetrical balance in the rock placement. As in nature, the rocks in the gardens did not perfectly line up in absolute symmetry. Asymmetry adds a dynamic element to art, whereas symmetry causes pieces to appear more static.

Moving on from the opening discussion, we modeled how to make a rock garden. We glued a few different-sized black construction paper rock prints onto a piece of white construction paper. We did a think-aloud as we glued down the paper rocks, talking about which sizes we chose and where we'd like to put them so the rock garden would have balance and space. We drew pencil lines between and around the rocks to represent water.

Then we asked students to design their own rock gardens. Each student received a piece of 9-by-12-inch white construction paper and a variety of construction paper rock cutouts. Students chose three to seven paper rock cutouts (no more than two jumbo sized) and placed them on their papers. The use of some small rocks helps visually balance the larger ones and contributes to asymmetry. When they were satisfied with their configurations, they glued the paper rocks onto their background sheets.

After they glued their paper rocks, students used pencils to draw line patterns around and between them. These line patterns represented water,

just as the lines in the sand of Japanese rock gardens represent water. The pieces were immediately striking because of the contrast between black and white and their interesting contour lines.

After sharing their art, students used a pencil to number the rocks in their garden from smallest to largest. Then we showed them the *Rock Garden* recording sheet. Their job was to estimate the number of pebbles it would take to cover each cutout. After they made their estimates, they needed to count and record the actual number of pebbles on each cutout. From there they calculated the difference between their estimate and the actual number. Finally, they had to find the total number of pebbles used to cover all the rock cutouts.

The mathematics proved rich and engaging for the students. Initially some of them expressed concern when their estimate did not match the actual number. We reminded them that estimates are about thinking and making reasonable mathematical guesses. It didn't matter if they were "right" or "closest." It just mattered that they used their brains and thought about the reasons for the numbers they chose.

The beauty of using the *Rock Garden* activity to estimate is that everything is irregular in shape. The rock patterns are curvy, and the pebbles have different sizes and shapes. It's rather obvious that there can't be one right answer and that the actual number will depend on the size and shape of the pebbles chosen. Many students made an effort to choose rocks that would get them closest to their estimates. This exercise was valuable and engaging because students used their visual, spatial skills to mentally manipulate the rocks and imagine how they would fill space. As Frannie MacKenzie, one of the teachers, noted, "Using real objects was very motivating for them."

Students shared their estimation strategies. Many used what they knew about covering the smaller rock cutouts to estimate how many pebbles it would take to cover a bigger one. Students also realized that rock cutouts of similar sizes probably needed about the same number of pebbles to cover them. As one student explained, "I think it's about seven again because it's about the same size as the last one." Students also compared the relative sizes of the rock cutouts to help with their estimates. Another student explained her thinking: "It has to fit at least eight because the smaller one fit eight."

The students had a range of strategies for finding the difference between their estimates and the actual number of pebbles they used. Many "counted up" to find the answer. Some used their fingers, and others used known facts. ("My estimate was six and the actual number is ten. I know six plus four equals ten, so the difference must be four.") One of the students even used negative numbers. He had guessed four rocks, but six actually fit, and he wrote *–2* as the difference between his estimate and the actual amount. When his next estimate was three over the actual amount, he wrote *+3*. When asked why he wrote *–2* for the first one, he explained that his estimate was "two under," so his estimate (four) minus the actual amount (six) was negative. When his estimate was larger than the actual amount, the difference was positive. Giving students freedom to find their own solution strategy allowed us to see what they knew and what number concepts they applied.

Finding the total number of pebbles proved to be another appropriate challenge for the students. They employed a variety of approaches that gave us valuable assessment information, such as counting the pebbles by ones, grouping the pebbles in tens, adding the numbers on their recording sheets, drawing pictures, using their fingers, using tally marks, and starting with the largest number and counting on from there. The range of methods impressed us and gave us much insight into students' number sense.

To close, the students shared some tips they had for finding the total number of pebbles. We chose to discuss this idea at the summary because it seemed to be the most challenging aspect of the investigation. When we asked if students had any other comments, we received positive feedback about the experience. Perhaps one of the second graders summed it up best when he said, "Mixing math and art is fun!"

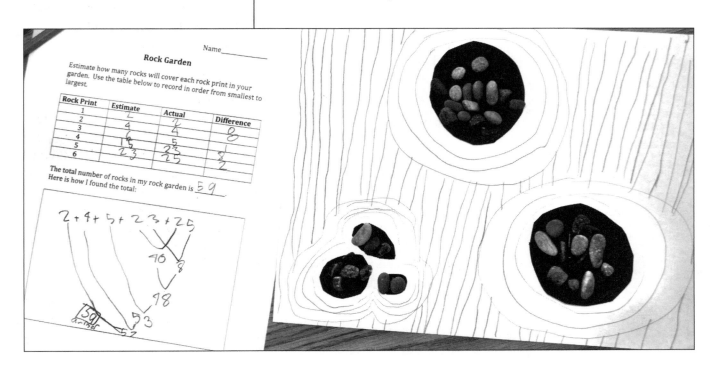

LESSON	# The *Bear*
Grade Level:	K–2, 3–5
Math Content Area:	Measurement
Math Overview:	This activity focuses on estimating the measurements of a large three-dimensional stone object. Younger students can do informal measurements and comparisons using nonstandard units. Older students get practice using standard units to estimate length, width, weight, and volume.
Guiding Questions:	**K–2** How does your size compare with this sculpture? How many of you would fit inside? Could this sculpture fit in our classroom? How can you tell? **3–5** How might you make reasonable estimates of this sculpture's dimensions? What benchmarks might help you?
Vocabulary:	compare, taller, shorter, wider, narrower, length, width, height, volume, weight
Materials:	paper, pencils, rulers, clipboards or hardback to work on, a stone structure or sculpture

We used a stone sculpture as a focal point for some open-ended, open-air mathematical investigations (more bear images are included on the CD that accompanies the book). When some third and fourth graders came to visit the UC–San Diego campus, we walked them over to see Tim Hawkinson's *Bear* sculpture. This huge stone teddy bear, composed of giant boulders, sits on a grassy patch among modern buildings. The students delighted in both the subject and its monumental size (see photo on next page).

We challenged the students to consider the visual, structural, and mathematical elements of the bear. We gave each one a clipboard with several pieces of paper and a pencil. The first page on the clipboard was a half sheet with some simple prompts:

Get to Know *Bear*
1. Draw *Bear*.
2. Draw *Bear* from a different perspective.
3. Estimate the length and width of the different pieces of *Bear*. Label the parts and their measurements.
4. Estimate the height of *Bear*.
5. Estimate the weight of *Bear*. Compare it with other things you know.
6. Write some questions you have about *Bear*.

These types of prompts also work well in a journal format (see Chapter 8, "The Journal"). They allowed students to practice measurement

and estimation skills in a real-world, fun context. Because the students were visiting *Bear* only one time on a field trip, we chose to give them several ways to interact with it at once. If a stone sculpture or structure is easily accessible from your school, you might choose to visit it more than once over a period of time and have students record their findings in a journal. Although it lacks the immediacy of a personal encounter, using a projected image of a sculpture or structure works for these types of activities as well.

We found that the prompts gave students different ways to perceive Bear and meaningfully interact with a sculpture. We "read" the world with our senses and filter it through the experience of our past perceptions. All sculpture and objects in space are perceived visually, but also spatially through our bodies. We compare and relate to objects in our physical environment initially with our own bodies. It is our primary system of understanding and comparing spatial relationships. Seeing something that is familiar but whose size, place, and context have been radically altered jars us from our everyday perceptions. We begin to question some of our basic assumptions about the world. What is hard and what is soft? How do we know this? Can a cuddly-looking toy be frightening? How big is big? Artists intentionally challenge our common perceptions. They invite us to encounter new aesthetic experiences.

LESSON

Rock Walls and Forms

Grade Level: K–2, 3–5

Math Content Area: Number and Operations, Measurement

Math Overview: Students participate in counting, adding, and measuring activities as they create rock walls for different landscapes. Students make predictions about extending their rock walls and about the number of rocks required to build walls of different dimensions.

Guiding Questions:

Number and Operations

How many rocks did you use to build your wall?

About how many rocks would it take to build a wall across your desk? Across the classroom?

Measurement

About how long is your rock wall? How can you tell?

Vocabulary: sum, total, addition, length, measure, landscape, spiral, perspective, plane

Materials: pebbles, colored pencils, paper, black markers, rock structures in landscape images

Start by showing students some images of landscapes with rock walls or forms. Smithson's *Spiral Jetty* makes an excellent example of this genre. Ask students what they notice. Also ask them to think about the purposes of the structures and how they might be constructed.

Have students pick a place—a local venue or a place they're familiar with through literature or geography lessons—and choose a rural landscape to draw. They don't need to make detailed drawings, but make sure they're aware of a few distinguishing features to include. For example, Ireland has rolling green hills with an occasional tree or building, whereas China's mountains are much more steep and angular, often bisected by rivers or gorges. Have a brief discussion about perspective in art and how to make a flat plane look three-dimensional. Layering planes or visible objects creates the illusion of three dimensions. Putting the farther objects down first and layering the closer objects on top of them accomplishes the layering effect. The closer objects are larger and overlap the things behind them in the viewer's field of vision.

Once students have sketched their landscapes, have them color them and write a few sentences about where their scene is and who lives there. Tell students they need to think about where rock structures might be useful or interesting in their landscape. Have them use pebbles to show where the rocks go. After they have laid out the rock wall, they need to estimate how many pebbles they used. After estimating, they find the actual number of pebbles. They then draw that number of rocks onto the landscape with a black marker.

Incorporate measurement by asking students to estimate the length of their walls. This task is challenging because most of the rock walls are curved. Students might estimate in nonstandard units such as paper clips or thumbprints. Alternatively, they can estimate in centimeters or inches.

Extend the activity by having students imagine and estimate the number of rocks it would take to build a wall or spiral that spans their tabletop. They can also estimate the length of the wall. Encourage students to use the data from their smaller rock walls as a benchmark for making estimates about the larger forms.

LESSON | Cave Paintings

Grade Level: | K–2, 3–5

Math Content Area: | Number and Operations

Math Overview: | This activity provides a unique context for creating and solving story problems. Highly adaptable, *Cave Paintings* can focus on any operation, and the number size can be adjusted based on the students' needs and prior experiences. By creating and illustrating their own story problems, students develop deeper understandings of operations and the contexts in which they are used.

Guiding Questions: | What is your story about?
How did you show the numbers on your cave painting?
How did you show the operation on your cave painting?

Vocabulary: | pictograph, symbol, operation, equation

Materials: | flat pieces of stone (remnants of sandstone flagstone work best and can be obtained at rock and masonry supply or garden and landscape supply stores), cotton swabs, sticks, tempera paint, newsprint, pencils, computation problems written on slips of paper or computation problems from the textbook, *Cave Painting Planning Sheet* (see appendix and CD), images of cave paintings

This activity requires several steps, so it's best to model an example with the whole class. Start by showing some images of cave paintings and pictographs. Ask students what they notice about these images. Emphasize the use of simple lines and shapes to convey important ideas and objects. Discuss the use of symbols in art and math. Shapes or pictures can represent a concept. Similarly, numbers are symbols that represent quantity.

Present an equation to the students. For younger grades it might be as simple as $4 + 3 = ?$. Older students might work with fractions, larger numbers, or more advanced operations such as multiplication or division. Write the equation on the whiteboard or on a large piece of newsprint. Ask students to think about stories that might match the equation. After they

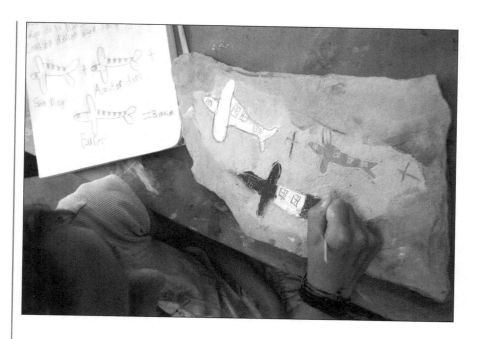

have generated a list of possible contexts, choose one to illustrate as an example. Use simple lines and shapes to draw the story problem.

After students understand the model, distribute equations for them to create cave paintings about. Use numbers and operations that focus on computation students are familiar with. Equations from the textbook might even be used. The activity can be differentiated by having different types or levels of equations to meet the needs of different students in the class.

Have students do a rough draft with paper and pencil first. The *Cave Painting Planning Sheet* helps students focus and refine their ideas before finalizing their work in stone (literally). When they are ready, students copy their paper drawings onto a piece of stone using cotton swabs dipped in tempera paint. Have them title their pieces.

As students share their cave paintings, others can give feedback and make predictions about what the story is about and what numbers and operations fit the story. These decorative pieces might also be sorted in ways to show different stories that describe the same equation. Although the paint isn't waterproof, the final product can be sprayed with a clear sealer to help preserve it. The flagstones make for a beautiful temporary garden or classroom floor installation.

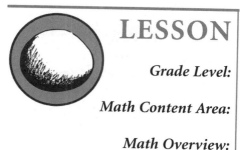

LESSON | Aquarium Rock Mosaics

Grade Level: 3–5

Math Content Area: Number and Operations, Geometry, Measurement

Math Overview: *Aquarium Rock Mosaics* give students practice using an area model to explore fractions and fractional relationships. Students apply their understanding of benchmarks and equivalent fractions to create accurate geometric representations of fractional pieces. They also find different combinations of fractions that total one whole. Opportunities to compare and order fractions arise as students divide and subdivide areas on a square. Additionally, students see how geometric shapes can be taken apart and recombined to make other shapes.

Guiding Questions:

Number and Operations

Which fractions are you showing? Where are they?

How did you divide your tile?

Which is the largest fraction? Which is the smallest? How many of the smallest make the largest?

Geometry

What shapes did you create by dividing your square?

What are the relationships among the shapes you created?

Measurement

What is the area of your mosaic tile?

What is the area of each color?

Vocabulary: fraction, area, divide, shape, mosaic

Materials: 4-by-4-inch paper squares, modeling clay rolled out into 4-by-4-inch tiles (approximately ¼ -inch thick), aquarium gravel (several different colors—we used blue, red, yellow, and black), containers for the gravel, sticks or bent paper clips to mark the clay, plastic spoons, paper plates to work on

This activity can get a bit messy, so it's best to cover tables before beginning. Although we undertook the lesson as a whole-class activity, it also makes sense to limit it to one table and have small groups rotate through. This activity can also be done by gluing aquarium rock onto commercially available tile. Low-fired or matte glaze tiles work best and can often be obtained

very inexpensively or sometimes donated from home-improvement or tile stores when there are closeouts or remainders.

We gave the students simple directions. Their task involved making a design that was one-half blue, one-eighth red, one-fourth yellow, and one-eighth black. First they sketched several designs on paper squares. They showed their designs to a partner to confirm that they indeed met the fraction criteria. This process of creating several design options served various purposes. It stretched their thinking about different ways to represent the same fractions. It also mirrored the process that artists use when considering their work. Furthermore, it ensured that the representations had mathematical accuracy before creating the actual tile.

After students had sketched a few options, they chose their favorite to transfer onto a clay tile and used a toothpick to outline their designs. Then they spooned the appropriate color of gravel onto the various parts. The spoon also served as a tool to press the gravel firmly into the clay so it wouldn't shake off.

Students showed great enthusiasm for this activity. The opportunity to work with clay and to design their own tiles proved very motivating. Many students not only sought geometric solutions to the fraction task, but also pushed themselves to create pictures and images that met the fraction criteria.

LESSON | Stone Buildings

Grade Level: K–2, 3–5

Math Content Area: Geometry, Measurement

Math Overview: This activity requires students to transform two-dimensional pictures into three-dimensional representations. It helps them name, build, and compare two- and three-dimensional shapes. They also recognize and describe their attributes. Additionally, students explore the results of combining, subdividing, and transforming shapes.

Guiding Questions:

Geometry

What is the shape of the building?
What smaller shapes is the building made of?
Why might the builders have chosen this design?

Measurement

How might you estimate the length, width, and height of this building?
How do the dimensions of your model of the building compare with the actual building? How can you tell?

Vocabulary: pattern, shape, texture, two-dimensional, three-dimensional, base, pyramid, prism, cylinder, proportion, scale, similar, additive process, subtractive process, façade

Materials: images of stone structures, clay, 6-by-6-inch cardboard foundation squares, clay tools such as toothpicks, paper clips, old pencils

We started by showing students pictures of a variety of stone buildings. This sparked an interesting discussion about where the buildings might be, what they might be used for, who might live in them, and why people would choose to make buildings out of stone. The discussion touched on history and culture and the many ways people have used the same material in different places for different purposes. We also talked about the shapes and sizes of the buildings and asked students to think about how the structures were built and why the builders would choose a particular design. Students noticed some patterns in the structures, which proved helpful as well.

From here pairs of students chose a picture of a stone building to copy. We gave them modeling clay to use rather than individual stones. Their job was to create a version of their building that would fit on the 6-by-6-inch cardboard foundation we provided. Some pairs chose to mold individual bricks or stones from their clay and build their structure accordingly. Other students molded the clay into a shell of the building and then used toothpicks or pencils to etch stone markings onto the façade.

Whether students created façades, crafted individual clay stones (additive process), or carved details out of a large form (subtractive process), they grappled with the same mathematical concepts. *Where should I start? What's the best way to put this together so it will be sturdy? How can I make my clay replica look like the picture I'm copying?* Issues of scale, proportion, and similarity naturally arose from the work.

As a follow-up we asked students to estimate the length, width, and height of the original building. In many cases these estimates had little data to rely on, so we allowed for any reasonable guess that had a mathematical rationale. Students shared a new awareness and appreciation for the built environment and the math involved in real-world problem solving.

CHAPTER 5

PAPER

P aper: there's plenty of it around, although teachers often have to budget its usage. One ream of copy paper yields 500 sheets. That means hundreds of opportunities to do math and create art right there. Construction paper is also a staple at most elementary schools and can be procured relatively cheaply if it's not readily available. Paper is commonly used for both math and art.

We found many ways to use paper: for collages, jewelry, sculptures, and more. This chapter describes some ideas for doing creative things with paper that incorporate math and art.

PAPER AND THE MATHEMATICS

Paper offers lots of informal measurement opportunities. Younger students can use pieces of paper to estimate and measure length, width, perimeter, or area. They can measure with nonstandard units such as paper clips, cubes, or even thumbprints. Ask older students how many 3-by-3-inch squares can be cut from a 9-by-12-inch sheet of construction

ACTIVITY	GRADES	NUMBER AND OPERATIONS	ALGEBRA	GEOMETRY	MEASUREMENT	DATA ANALYSIS AND PROBABILITY
Fraction Montage	K–2	✓		✓		
Polygon Pictures	K–2			✓		
Still-Life Collages	K–2, 3–5			✓		
Paper Folding	3–5	✓	✓	✓		✓
Paper Bead Necklaces	3–5	✓	✓			
Tessellations and M. C. Escher	3–5			✓	✓	
Paper Bag Sculptures	3–5				✓	

paper. Then ask them to figure out how many 3-by-3-inch squares they can get from a 12-by-18-inch piece of construction paper.

Paper is perfect for folding and cutting. A sheet of paper is a two-dimensional plane, but through folding or cutting and taping, it becomes three-dimensional. The patterns created by folding paper and the shapes created by cutting paper provide multiple explorations of algebra, fractions, geometry, and measurement concepts. And how refreshing for students to associate math and paper with something other than worksheets.

PAPER AND THE ART CONNECTIONS

Paper is one of the oldest and most common materials used in art. Records date its earliest production back to around AD 100 in China. Paper is made from the fibers of several different kinds of plants mixed with water, beaten flat and allowed to dry. The invention and mechanization of paper changed everything. Paper allowed humans to easily record, reproduce, and share information, language, business, and art. For thousands of years the development of commerce, culture, and civilization has depended on paper.

Paper comes in many sizes, weights, and colors. Mechanization made it possible to produce large quantities of consistent size and quality, but paper really hasn't changed much in the last 2,000 years. It is one of the earliest technological advances to remain in continuous use. It is difficult to imagine any business, classroom, or household in which you won't find paper. Different kinds of paper serve different purposes. There's graph paper, tracing paper, copy paper, drawing paper, carbon paper, wallpaper, butcher paper, wrapping paper, construction paper, newspaper, watercolor paper, and sandpaper. The list goes on.

Choosing the right kind of paper for a given art activity is an important place to start. Some papers hold up better to paint, such as watercolor or construction paper. The texture of some papers is too rough for drawing. Some papers are heavy and more durable, making it easier for younger students to cut, roll, or form (construction paper). Some are used to help transfer images (tracing, graph, carbon papers). Rosin paper, durable enough to protect floors during construction projects, is water resistant and reusable. It is available at most hardware stores and is perfect for covering tables during art projects.

Paper is an essential medium in the history of art. It is difficult to imagine an artist who didn't begin by making marks on paper. Artists use paper in every way imaginable. Paper is cut, collaged, folded, sewn, glued, stapled, rolled, and painted. Artists create their own paper from pulp and cast it into forms. Many artists work with paper and other media in the genre of book arts. Almost all artists use sketchbooks to work out and record their ideas and to make preliminary drawings for paintings and larger projects.

Dozens of different printing processes use paper as their medium. It is used in the printing of photographs, lithographs, etchings, and silk screens. Posters on paper are a popular and inexpensive art form. Handmade political posters and graphic advertisements are produced on paper in countries worldwide.

Many countries have traditional arts that use paper. China boasts a tradition of cut paper art called Jianzhi. Artists fold colored paper several times and use scissors to cut it into elaborate designs, an intricate process similar to cutting paper dolls. These symmetrical designs often depict traditional Chinese scenes, landscapes, plants, animals, and cultural symbols. In ancient China and Japan important stories and historical events were recorded in ink paintings on large paper scrolls. Paper scrolls provided a perfect material for easy transport and storage of information and images.

From as far back as the thirteenth century illuminated manuscripts played an important role in recording historical events and religious doctrine in Europe, Asia, and North Africa. Paper manuscripts typically featured gold or silver paint and stylized calligraphy. These elaborate and highly detailed paintings, accompanied by hand-scribed text, were bound into books.

Many kinds of paper can be used for folding. Wrapping paper with different patterns on each side is fun to use for folding and collage. Almost any paper can be used to create a collage—art made from layers of paper glued together. Colored paper and magazines are perfect collage materials. Collage is an easy activity to extend to multiple sessions, a fun medium to paint on, and a great way to recycle leftover paper of all kinds.

Origami is the traditional Japanese technique of folding paper. Today origami artists create an amazing array of forms from a square of paper. Students love the challenge of creating traditional and unique paper art forms. In this chapter they explore folding paper to predict and create polygons and sculptural pieces.

M. C. Escher's graphic art on paper showed the depth and potential of this simple medium. He used paper for more than 2,000 drawings and sketches. His highly technical drawings featured fantasy worlds with complex and often impossible landscapes and architectural structures. Known for his tessellating drawings, Escher's work combines key elements in geometry with art elements such as balance, symmetry, and pattern.

Installation Art emerged in the 1970s and became popular in the 1990s. An immersive quality characterizes the Installation genre. Artists create entire environments that surround the viewer in a multisensory experience. In 2004 Ann Hamilton created an installation titled *Corpus*, using light, sound, and paper. In a huge light-filled old factory building, she had millions of sheets of translucent paper drop from the ceiling over a period of months. The paper drifted to the floor in piles while the room was filled with voices from speakers hanging from the rafters. Her 1994 piece titled *Linement* was part performance, part Installation Art. Here the printed text from books was cut into ribbons and wound into balls. She used words on paper as an art material, making it tactile and transforming it from two to three dimensions.

Kara Walker uses paper exclusively in her work. Her work focuses on the history of slavery and of power and privilege in American culture. She is known for her large "wallpaper" scenes of cutout black paper silhouettes. Her work is narrative without using words, rich in story and cultural history, and created only from cut black paper.

Andy Warhol used commercial techniques of photography and printmaking. He was one of the first artists to blend pop culture, commercial art, and fine art. He made much of his work in multiples on paper. He also printed on paper shopping bags, deliberately challenging the historical constraints of what materials and images were considered fine art.

Tara Donovan is an emerging artist recognized for her work using large quantities of everyday common materials in large installations. She uses materials such as paper cups, drinking straws, rolls of translucent paper, and Mylar (a metallic paper) to build sculptural objects and create whole environments. Her room-sized installation of layered and stacked torn roofing paper recalls a mountainous and distant landscape. She has created wondrous sculptures from materials as simple as paper plates.

Romare Bearden was an important and prolific artist dedicated throughout his life to social justice and the promotion of African American culture. He was born in North Carolina in 1911 and moved to New York City to study education. An art editor for magazines and a published essayist in humanities journals, he also worked for years as a social worker in New York. His artwork focused on the life, culture, and social environment of everyday people from his neighborhood. He worked in many mediums, but is best known for his visually rich multimedia collages. He sometimes incorporated photographic images into his collages, a technique known as photomontage. He also authored many scholarly works about African American culture and a children's book about the Civil War, which he illustrated. In 1987, the year before he died, he received the National Medal of Arts.

Paper Art Vocabulary: abstraction, background, calligraphy, collage, cool color, Cubism, etching, foreground, form, graphic art, illuminated manuscript, Installation Art, Jianzhi, layout, lithographs, medium, mixed media, monochromatic, origami, perspective, photomontage, portfolio, positive/negative space, primary color, printmaking, sculpture, secondary color, shape, silk screen, still life, tessellation, texture, three-dimensional, two-dimensional, volume, warm color

THE PAPER LESSONS

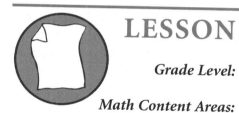

LESSON | Fraction Montage

Grade Level: K–2

Math Content Areas: Number and Operations, Geometry

Math Overview: This activity helps students solidify the concept of fractions as parts of a whole. Through a visual, geometric model, *Fraction Montage* familiarizes students with representations of common fractions.

Guiding Questions:

Number and Operations

What does one-fourth look like? How can you show fourths?

Geometry

What shapes do you see inside these other shapes?

Vocabulary: circle, rectangle, half, fourth, horizontal, vertical, equivalent

Materials: rectangles and circles of construction paper (from 9-by-12-inch sheets) folded into fourths or paper plates divided into fourths, glue, buttons, packing peanuts, magazine pages, toothpicks, straws, stickers, washers, stamps, cotton balls, markers, watercolors, scrapbook paper, tempera paint, and any other supplies that work for gluing or covering parts of the construction paper

Michelle Jimenez and Danielle Zdunich implemented this activity to integrate visual art into the study of fractions with their first graders. They focused on the fraction one-fourth. Kindergarten classes might start with one-half instead.

First, they gave students a choice of three different pieces of paper that were all folded into fourths. The paper choices were a circle, a rectangle folded once horizontally and once vertically, or a rectangle folded vertically twice. They reviewed the name of the fraction, one-fourth, and talked about why all these different folding arrangements yielded fourths. Then they gave students a moment to decide which one-fourth configuration they wanted to work with. They encouraged students to choose different options so that there would be a variety of art designs among the group.

Students then chose decorations for each one-fourth section of their paper. Each section had to involve a different art material. They could choose from buttons, cotton balls, markers, watercolors, scrapbook paper, and tempera paint. Connecting arts vocabulary (*collage, mixed media, two-dimensional, three-dimensional, layout*) to the students' work and decision making helped students explicitly experience the overlap of art and math. Michelle and Danielle put each group of art supplies at a separate table so that students had working stations. They allowed a maximum of four students at each supply table to keep it manageable.

The students took full advantage of all the materials and found distinctive ways to represent one-fourth, whether with scraps of paper, marker, or cotton balls. They took their time with the activity and were careful in their design of each fractional part. Because each section of the paper had to be decorated with different materials, each piece stood out clearly yet still remained part of the whole. Students also had to represent the fraction numerically to demonstrate their understanding of the symbolic notation. They didn't decorate any two sections of their "whole" paper the same, thus showing their understanding of equivalent fractional pieces in very creative, visual ways. Exploring the qualities of different materials, categorizing by shape, texture, color, size, and making choices about placement and layout are important artistic skills young students develop through this work.

The children's final products impressed Michelle and Danielle. It was obvious that the students took tremendous pride in their work. After the students finished their pieces, Michelle and Danielle told them to make sure each fourth of their art was labeled with the fraction ¼. After their pieces had dried, students shared them with the class. They pointed out each one-fourth and told what materials they used. Then the art was posted in the room for classmates and visitors to view.

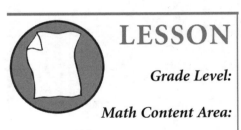

LESSON | Polygon Pictures

Grade Level: K–2

Math Content Area: Geometry

Math Overview: *Polygon Pictures* challenges students to find ways to put shapes together to create new shapes. In doing so students recognize and name different polygons and learn about their attributes. The activity also requires students to use academic language to describe the relative positions of polygons.

Guiding Questions: What happens when you put different shapes together?
How can you describe where the shapes are?

Vocabulary: square, triangle, rectangle, trapezoid, hexagon, circle, above, below, next to, to the right of, to the left of

Materials: white 9-by-12-inch construction paper, colored construction paper shapes (use *Polygon Template*; see appendix and CD), glue

This activity is similar to the *Polygon Portraits* activity in the chapter on the face, which explains and connects the lesson to such art terms such as *Abstract* and *Cubism*. Terri Kim implemented *Polygon Pictures* to allow her first graders to explore geometric shapes and describe proximity, position, and direction while creating works of art. She started the lesson by going over the names of basic shapes and making an illustrated word bank for the students. She included words such as *square, rectangle, triangle, trapezoid, pentagon,* and *hexagon.* Creating a word bank for key vocabulary gave students the language support they needed. It also gave English language learners the extra support they needed to participate in the lesson from beginning to end. The word bank was not an exhaustive list, but rather a few key words that Terri thought were important for the lesson.

Next Terri modeled how to make a simple bird using different shapes. She made sure to tell students that the edges of the shapes need to be touching and were not allowed to overlap. She defined these parameters so that students would clearly be able to see how different shapes fit together to make new shapes. She also wanted them to be able to use direction terms such as *next to, to the left of, above,* and so on. Overlapping shapes would complicate things.

She made the bird with different shapes and glued them to a piece of white paper, thus modeling what the students would be doing independently. Then she modeled how to describe the shapes and their positions. For example, she pointed to different polygons and said, "The triangle is to the left of the squares. This trapezoid is below the squares. This trapezoid is above the squares. This trapezoid is to the right of the squares."

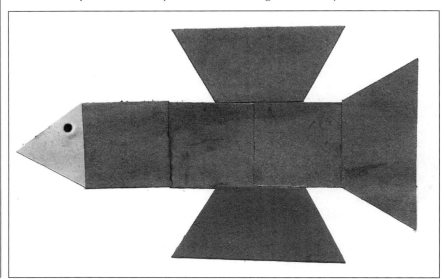

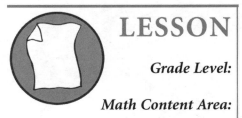

Terri went over the directions with the students once more and sent them to their tables to make their own art pieces. As the students went to their seats, Terri handed each one a piece of white construction paper. She also gave each table of students a plastic zippered bag full of cutout shapes to share.

The students had time to make their own artwork using the different shapes. They really enjoyed the activity, especially because of the art element. It gave them the opportunity to explore their creativity, and they produced some very interesting pieces. They excitedly discussed the different things they had made using different shapes. After they were finished gluing and making their art, Terri instructed students to share their piece with a partner and talk about its different shapes and positions. She wanted to give them oral practice, which proved very beneficial. As she walked around to monitor progress, Terri asked questions such as the following:

What shapes did you use?
Can you tell me about your picture?
Where are your shapes located?

The students learned the names of some more shapes (especially *hexagon* and *trapezoid*). Some of them referred to the illustrated word bank in the front of the classroom. This visual model helped them practice reading and saying the names of the shapes.

To summarize the lesson Terri had a few students share their pictures with the class. They accurately named the different shapes in their pieces. The students also learned how to describe where the shapes were in terms of position and directionality. For example, one student said, "The hexagon is next to the square, and I used a triangle for the head, which is on top of the trapezoid."

At the end Terri engaged the whole class by asking them to show a thumbs-up if they had used certain shapes in their own artwork. ("Thumbs-up if you used a square." "Thumbs-up if you used a hexagon.") Last, she asked them to think of one thing they liked about the activity. One student shared, "This is fun because you can make anything out of shapes."

To extend the lesson Terri thought of adding a writing component. She had the students write a few sentences that described their picture in order to continue to reinforce the vocabulary as well as to review the position and location of the shapes. The writing element helped with management, because early finishers worked on the writing portion after they finished creating their art piece.

LESSON Still-Life Collages

Grade Level: K–2, 3–5

Math Content Area: Geometry

Math Overview: In *Still-Life Collages* students create two-dimensional representations of a three-dimensional model. They gain practice in recognizing polygons and seeing ways in which they can be put together and taken apart to make other polygons. Older students encounter issues of perspective, angles, and geometric vocabulary. This activity pushes students to look at complex, three-dimensional shapes (a bouquet of flowers) and identify component shapes within the more complex composite image. They transfer the components of the three-dimensional object to a two-dimensional plane— a piece of paper.

Guiding Questions: **K–2**

What shapes do you know?

Where do you see those shapes?

3–5

How can you combine shapes to create new shapes?

How might you create a two-dimensional representation of a three-dimensional object?

Vocabulary: triangle, rhombus, circle, pentagon, hexagon, square, rectangle, negative space, background, foreground, perspective, two-dimensional, three-dimensional

Materials: 9-by-12-inch or 12-by-18-inch colored construction paper, construction paper and magazine shape cutouts (use the *Polygon Template* in the appendix or on the CD, or have students cut out their own), glue, bunch of flowers in a vase or container

A still life is a portrait of inanimate objects, usually a vase of flowers, food, books, or objects typically found in the home. The still life has always been an important subject for artists in painting, drawing, and photography. This activity takes the traditional subject matter and employs an approach that engages every student while integrating important mathematical ideas. Students use construction paper shapes to create a still-life collage of a vase of flowers provided as a model. They can look at the negative space between the flowers, leaves, and stems to consider what shapes make up that negative space as well.

Cynthia Caputo implemented the activity with her second graders. With her young students, Cynthia placed the vase of flowers in front of the room so that they all had a relatively similar view.

First, Cynthia had the students take some time to carefully observe the vase of flowers at the front of the classroom. They talked about what they saw, and Cynthia connected their observations to important vocabulary terms (*shape, triangle, square, rectangle, circle, oval, angle, line, petal, stem, leaf*). She wrote those words on the board as they arose. Then the students cut out shapes from different-colored construction paper.

Cynthia encouraged students to see how some shapes fit together to make new shapes. This investigation prepared them for the collage activity while addressing a crucial concept in geometry. Then students took their shapes and created still-life collages. They glued the construction paper shapes to another larger piece of paper that served as the background. They used the word *background* to describe the large piece of

paper and *foreground* to describe where the vase fit. Once the students had access to the materials and began working, they naturally began talking to each other about the shapes and using the proper names for each one. They looked at each other's artwork, yet still continued to make their own pieces in their own ways. Students appreciated the openness of the task and the uniqueness of the products. They made comments such as "Wow, yours looks so different from mine!" "Oh, that is so cool! Come look at mine," and "Look at how many new shapes I used!"

After creating their masterpieces the students talked with partners about what they had made, how they had made it, and why. As the students shared their artwork, they displayed a sense of excitement and accomplishment. Cynthia guided them to use the academic language they had generated earlier in the lesson. Having the vocabulary on the board proved very helpful. The students were able to review their mathematical knowledge of geometrical shapes. They discussed the different shapes, what they looked like, and how everything is made up of shapes, as well as how they could piece them together to make a vase of flowers. They also learned about different perspectives in art. They realized that no two people see a still life or any picture in the same way.

Upper-grade students can approach this activity with a focus on perspective. The flowers can be placed in the middle of the room so students have completely different views of the same object. This situation can lead to interesting discussions about angles, perspective, and spatial coordinates. Also, older students might mix in torn construction paper shapes and wadded tissue paper, adding layers of texture and visual interest to this activity while being challenged to create shapes without scissors.

Students might also try to create a sculptural still life by using rolled and folded construction paper. Adding shapes from magazine pages that include parts of photos and text provides additional interesting visual connections. Another follow-up activity entails making rubbings from still-life collages. Students use shapes cut from thick tagboard or index cards. They glue these shapes onto a larger piece of tagboard to create a textured collage. Then they lay a piece of thinner white paper (copy paper works fine) over the collage and lightly color over the paper with a crayon. Displaying the monochromatic collage next to its colored rubbing shows the striking effects different media and techniques have on the same subject.

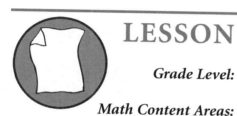

LESSON

Paper Folding

Grade Level: 3–5

Math Content Areas: Number and Operations, Algebra, Geometry, Data Analysis and Probability

Math Overview: In this *Paper Folding* investigation students create geometric models to investigate algebraic growth patterns. They use prediction and data organization to make sense of exponential growth.

Guiding Questions:

Number and Operations
Describe the number patterns you notice. What operations explain the patterns?

Algebra
What patterns do you notice?
What predictions can you make based on the patterns you see?

Geometry
Which shapes did you create by folding your paper?
Is it possible to get any other shapes? Tell how you know.
What are the results of folding different shapes in different ways?
What's the connection between the shapes and the number patterns?

Data Analysis and Probability
How does the T-table help you find patterns and make predictions?
Are there other ways you could display this same data?
Look closely at the data on your recording sheet. Do you see any patterns? Describe them.

Vocabulary: horizontal, vertical, diagonal, exponent, pattern, prediction

Materials: 3-by-3-inch squares of white construction paper, *Paper Folding Challenge* reproducible (see appendix and CD), pencil, 6-by-6-inch white construction paper squares, markers or colored pencils, black markers for outlining

Begin the lesson by holding up a paper square. Tell students you are going to fold it in half horizontally. Ask them what the new shape will be. Students should be able to tell you with relative ease that it's a rectangle. Then ask

them to tell you how many rectangles you'll have when you unfold the paper. Again, the students will know there are two rectangles within the folded square. Start a table on the board:

# folds	# shapes	shape
0	1	☐ square
1	2	▯ rectangles
2	4	⊞ squares
3	8	▦ rectangles

Have students predict how many shapes you'll have within the original square when you fold it in half and then fold it in half again. Add that data to the table. Students continue to make predictions about the number of shapes when the square is folded three and four times. Ask students how they made their predictions. Some will notice patterns on the T-table, whereas others will refer to the visual image of the folded square. Emphasize that there are several approaches to making these predictions and that some students approach the task numerically and others do it visually. This point is crucial as students continue to develop their sense that mathematics and visual arts can be connected in many helpful ways. Continue with folding three and four times and add the new data to the chart each time.

As the table grows, prompt students to notice patterns. Highlight the relationship between the number of folds and the number of shapes. These numbers grow exponentially by the powers of two. Model the symbolic notation on the board as you connect the symbols to the folded paper.

$$2^0 = 1$$
$$2^1 = 2$$
$$2^2 = 4$$
$$2^3 = 8$$

This important number pattern will recur throughout students' studies of mathematics and science. Explicit instruction and an accessible visual model will aid students in both recognizing and applying this pattern when it inevitably rises again.

Next pose a challenge for students to try at their table. Give them a paper square to fold in half—horizontally, vertically, or diagonally. They predict what shape they'll get by combining different types of half folds. Then students explore different ways to fold their squares in half and then

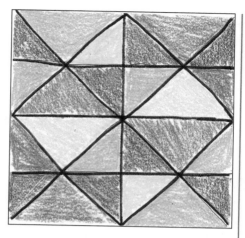

in half again, recording results on their recording sheets. The recording sheets help them organize their work and see the connection between the numeric and geometric representations. This investigation is open-ended. The only rule is that they must fold their squares in half somehow each time.

Students can follow up their paper-folding investigations with some writing. After they have created and recorded their new folding patterns, they can answer some of the guiding questions. Another option is to use these processing questions as prompts for a whole-class discussion. A whole-class discussion serves as an effective prewriting activity. Students have more ideas and language to employ in their writing when they've talked about the subject first.

Students can also show their recording sheets to partners, who then try to re-create the shapes and patterns by following the descriptions on the sheet. The partners can initial the far right column of the recording sheet each time they successfully re-create a shape pattern.

To further extend the activity, have students pick their favorite folded square from their recording sheet and copy it onto a 6-by-6-inch square. To outline each shape within the square they need to trace over the fold lines using a dark marker. Then they decorate each shape outlined in the square. These decorated squares can be used for follow-up fraction activities. Students can estimate and explain what fraction of the whole square various shapes are. The colorful squares can also be used to make a quilt or border in the classroom.

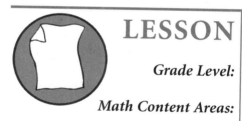

LESSON | Paper Bead Necklaces

Grade Level: 3–5

Math Content Areas: Number and Operations, Algebra

Math Overview: In designing and making paper bead necklaces students encounter different number patterns and representations. They deal with factors and multiples as they plan and design their necklaces.

Guiding Questions:

Number and Operations

What's the connection between your number pattern and the bead pattern?

Algebra

What number patterns do you see? Can you extend the pattern and make predictions beyond what you see?

Vocabulary: multiple, factor, odd, even, pattern, predict

Materials: red, blue, yellow, and green construction paper bead strips (or any four colors of your choice); pencils; tape; crayons matching the colors of the bead strips; roll of elastic string; *Paper Bead Recording Sheet* (see appendix and CD)

To begin the lesson with Kathrina Mendoza's third graders we showed some photos of beads. Students viewed and discussed the features and composition of a variety of beads. The images helped them make historical, geographical, and cultural connections. They looked at commercially made beads as well as beads made in Africa and by Native Americans. We also looked at the beaded bracelets and hair ornaments that belonged to some of the students in the class.

Part of our bead talk included a discussion of the use of patterns in beadwork. We easily segued into a discussion of number patterns. Students shared number patterns they knew:

Odd numbers
Even numbers
Multiples of two
Counting by fives

Students then chose a number pattern to represent on their *Paper Bead Recording Sheet.* We instructed the students to color all the numbers that fit their pattern with a red crayon. Students shared their red patterns on the sheets.

From there we told them they could choose blue, yellow, or green to color the other numbers on their planning sheets. We left this part of the task open. They could choose whichever other designated colors they wanted and could color in a pattern or not. The important part was having the pattern numbers in red so they'd be easily identifiable.

We prompted them to use mathematical and arts vocabulary to describe what they saw. How many primary and secondary colored beads did they plan to use? Would their necklaces be mostly warm or cool colors?

We then modeled making a paper bead. We worked together to create the bead, because we suspected it would be a two-person job for most of the students. We took a strip of the cut construction paper and rolled it

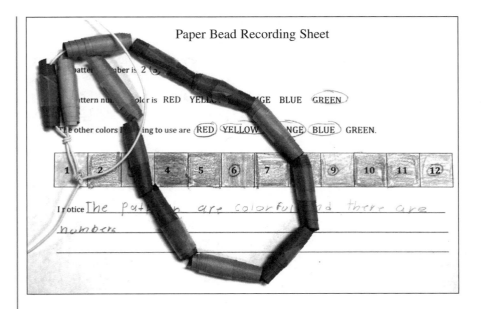

Paper Bead Recording Sheet

around a pencil, beginning with the wider end of the strip. When the paper was rolled around the pencil, we secured the narrow, outside end with a piece of tape. Then we slid the bead off the pencil.

We instructed the students to make fifteen to twenty colored beads to match the pattern they had created on their sheet. After they made their beads, they strung them in pattern order on a length of elastic string to make a necklace.

Students delighted in their creations. Many wore them to recess and looked forward to giving them as gifts to family members when they got home. In showing the necklaces to the rest of the class, we emphasized patterns and challenged students to guess which number pattern the red beads represented on different necklaces.

LESSON

Tessellations and M. C. Escher

Grade Level: 3–5

Math Content Areas: Geometry, Measurement

Math Overview: This activity presents students with the occasion to explore the results of sliding, rotating, and flipping two-dimensional shapes. Students also explore the results of subdividing and transforming shapes into other shapes. Measuring area is a natural extension to this project.

Guiding Questions:
Geometry
What will happen as you slide, rotate, or flip your shape?
Can you predict which shapes will tessellate and which will not? How?
Measurement
How can you figure out how many of your shapes you'll need to cover the entire surface?

Vocabulary: | tessellate, slide, rotate, pattern, tiling, symmetry, space, shape, plane, area

Materials: | paper, pattern blocks, index cards, construction paper, scissors, tape

Margaret Hayes taught this lesson to her bilingual fourth graders. She developed a sequence of lessons that helped students understand and create tessellations by exploring M. C. Escher's work. Third-grade teachers might skip the last part of the sequence if it seems too challenging for their students.

Margaret began by showing her students two of M. C. Escher's pieces—*Sky and Water 1* and *Metamorphosis*—and had them tell what they noticed. She focused on the tessellating or tiling aspect—that the same shape could be placed together repeatedly with no space between to cover the area. She then had students look for tiling or tessellating shapes in the classroom. The students noticed the ceiling tiles and some patterns on clothing that fit the criteria. She connected the tessellating shapes to the concept of area and covering a plane surface.

From there she instructed students to consider a set of pattern blocks. She asked them to make predictions about how different pattern blocks might tessellate. This exercise tapped into students' spatial visualization skills. Students then explored the pattern blocks on their tables and tried to completely cover the area of their desktops by using the same pattern block repeatedly. To extend the exploration they created new shapes by combining pattern blocks and checked to see if their new shapes tessellated.

After students had a firm grasp of the rules for a tessellation, they created their own unique tessellating designs. Each student received an index card to cut and tape into a new shape. Margaret modeled how to cut the index card in two pieces and slide one of the pieces up to the edge of the other piece. By taping those two pieces together, Margaret created a new tessellating shape.

Students then tested their shape by trying to tile a piece of paper with it. They traced the shape repeatedly and then named the pattern they created. They also wrote about how they knew it was tessellation. As a challenge some students created tessellating shapes that involved more than one cut and slide.

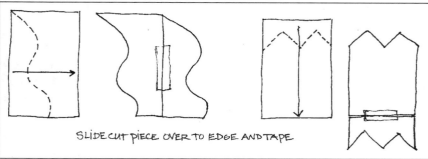

SLIDE CUT PIECE OVER TO EDGE AND TAPE

LESSON

Grade Level:

Math Content Area:

Math Overview:

Guiding Questions:

Vocabulary:

Materials:

Paper Bag Sculptures

3–5

Measurement

The *Paper Bag Sculptures* present students with practice in estimating and measuring the length, width, height, volume, and surface area of irregular shapes. They develop measurement strategies and use appropriate benchmarks to make their estimates.

How can you estimate the length, height, width, surface area, and volume of an irregular shape?

What measurement tools can help you with your estimates?

length, width, height, volume, surface area, shape, negative space, estimate

two paper bags per student, scissors, tape, stapler, rulers, cubes (cm or other), *Paper Bag Sculptures* recording sheet (see appendix and CD)

We used brown paper lunch bags for this lesson. The activity had two phases. First, students opened their bags and placed them upright on the table in front of them. Their job was to measure and record the dimensions

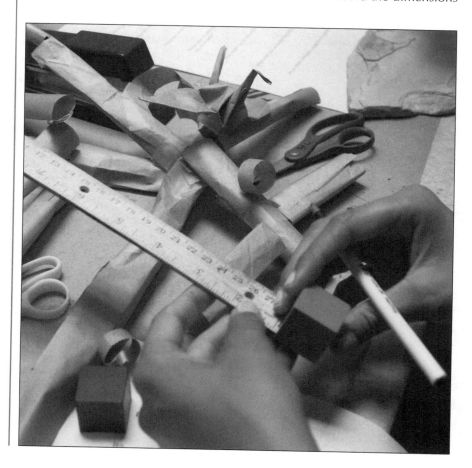

of their paper bag. We modeled where each of these dimensions resided on the bag. We also asked the students how they might use the cubes to help find the surface area and volume of the bag. They talked about filling the bag with cubes to find the volume. The notion of "stamping" a cube around the bag provided a way to think about surface area. Students also noticed that the paper bag's faces consisted of rectangles, so if they could find the area of each rectangular face, they could add those areas together to find the surface area. After students understood their measuring job, they got to work.

Next students used their second paper bag to create a freestanding sculpture. They used scissors and tape to reshape their bag into a new design. They needed to use all pieces of the bag, but it was fine to have pieces overlapping. Once the students had their new sculptures, they needed to compare them with their original bags.

We had them do the measurement comparisons in two ways. First, they needed to estimate whether they thought each dimension of their new sculpture was greater than or less than that of the original bag. Then they needed to estimate the measurements for their sculpture. The recording sheet helped them organize this information.

Because many of the new sculptures had irregularly shaped pieces and interior spaces, the estimates were challenging. Does interior space count as part of the surface area? What about curved and tubelike parts? We resolved some of the questions by having students imagine that their sculptures were completely solid and measure accordingly.

Finally, we had the students sketch their sculpture on the back of their recording sheets. This exercise gave them practice moving from three-dimensional to two-dimensional models and also forced them to consider issues of perspective and changing volumes.

Students used the recording sheets to reflect on the activity as well. They learned quite a bit. One student noted, "I learned the importance of estimation for oddly shaped objects. I learned that the same materials could represent different volumes and surface areas." Another student remarked, "I had to think about what the volume would be in my new sculpture because of the overlaps and cuts and loose parts."

All in all, this proved to be a challenging and motivating activity for the students. They confronted issues of estimation and measurement through interacting with their own original works of art.

CHAPTER 6

THE SHOE

You *know* your students will be prepared for these activities. As long as they arrive at school wearing shoes, they're ready to go. Shoes are very basic objects, literally grounding us and connecting us to the earth. They are essential to most of our daily lives. Although they are a fundamental part of our garb, shoes provide an amazing variety of styles, colors, purposes, and components. This variety gives teachers a myriad of ways to integrate shoes into meaningful, creative, engaging activities.

Depending on your geographic region and the season, the types of shoes your students wear will vary. Keep this in mind as you plan your lessons. We live in Southern California, so on any given day most of our elementary students are wearing some sort of sneaker or tennis shoe. If your school has a prescribed shoe as part of the school uniform or you find there isn't much variation in the shoes in your classroom, you can ask students to bring a shoe from home that they will use for the sequence of lessons. The shoe from home doesn't have to be theirs; they can borrow one from a family member. You can even provide a prompt that challenges

ACTIVITY	GRADES	NUMBER AND OPERATIONS	ALGEBRA	GEOMETRY	MEASUREMENT	DATA ANALYSIS AND PROBABILITY
All About My Shoe	K–2, 3–5	✓			✓	
Shoe Comparing	K–2		✓			
Shoe Sorting	K–2		✓			
Shoe Graphing	K–2, 3–5					✓
Masking Tape Shoes	3–5			✓		
Shoe Rubbings	3–5		✓			

them to "find an interesting shoe at home and bring it to class. Make sure it's okay with the adult in charge. You will return the shoe unharmed when we're finished with our activities."

If your students need to take their shoes off for the activities you do, you might want to let them know ahead of time so they can choose shoes (and socks) accordingly. Also consider the weather. You might prefer to have your students keep their shoes on if sweaty socks or bare feet might interfere with the focus. We think shoes are the perfect context for integrating math and visual arts. We encourage you to put on your sneakers and jump in.

THE SHOE AND THE MATHEMATICS

Why are shoes so perfect for integrating math and visual arts? Well, first of all, shoe designers consider all the elements of visual arts when creating their products: color, pattern, line, and balance all play into how a shoe looks and who will find it appealing.

Shoes provide built-in measurement opportunities. Students get new shoes based on size and often must have their feet measured to figure out what size they are. Plus, shoes are fabulous, curved, three-dimensional objects with both positive and negative space to measure.

In addition to providing measurement opportunities, shoes have visual and numerical patterns that lend themselves nicely to graphing and algebra. A good shoe can take you a long way.

THE SHOE AND THE ART CONNECTIONS

The shoe as an art object has a long cultural history that is rich in metaphor. One can trace style and fashion, and social, economic, and regional cultural connections through shoes. Shoes are used as a metaphor to reflect our experience in common sayings such as "Walk a mile in my shoes" or "Those will be big shoes to fill." In the arts, shoes can act as a stand-in for people in stories about human events. Artists have employed the shoe to represent migration, personal experience, and social status. Visual artists and historians have used shoes to help us visualize the loss of human life in genocide and human rights abuses. We can imagine a wide range of human experience just by looking at different kinds of shoes (think of clown shoes, moccasins, Japanese wooden slats, and so on).

In the early 1970s contemporary artist Eleanor Antin created a series of photographs on postcards titled *100 Boots* that shows a group of one hundred boots in various locations. The postcards acted as both the art material and documentation of the project. She has referred to the series as a "pictorial novel" that arrived in the mail unannounced to thousands of people in different parts of the world.

Elizabeth Murray, an artist known for her whimsical, colorful, and dimensional paintings (paintings with pieces that protrude from the wall), was commissioned in 1996 to create a site-specific sculpture for the renowned Stuart Collection on the campus of University of California–San Diego. In a surrounding of eucalyptus trees she placed a giant cartoonish and festive *Red Shoe* that one can climb onto and inside. Scattered around the shoe, which looks as if it just walked into its place, are jewel-like sculptural objects.

Robert Rauschenberg is considered one of the most important American artists of the twentieth century. He is known for his early use of unlikely materials and found objects such as shoes, tennis balls, taxidermy,

and paint to create sculptures that he called "combines." Causing quite a stir in the art world in the early 1960s, he pioneered new techniques in printmaking and collage with low-tech processes such as simple rubbings, or printing from tire treads. He continued to have a long and influential career in the arts until his death in 2008.

René Magritte, a Belgian Surrealist artist, painted a pair of boots that morph into human feet with laces. There are sketches, photographs, and paintings by artists throughout history who have used shoes as a subject. Shoes from every culture and time period can be found in collections in the great museums around the world.

Shoe Art Vocabulary: collage, dimensional paintings, printing, rubbing, site-specific sculpture, Surrealism

THE SHOE LESSONS

LESSON — All About My Shoe

Grade Level: K–2, 3–5

Math Content Area: Number and Operations, Measurement

Math Overview: In *All About My Shoe* students investigate the physical features of their shoes and record details about shoe measurements. Students' estimates allow them to compare quantities and do some mental computation.

Guiding Questions:

K–2 Number and Operations
What are some ways to count and find out how many?
What tools can help with counting and finding out how much or how many?

K–2 Measurement
What parts of the shoe can we measure?
How can we measure different parts of a shoe?

3–5 Number and Operations
How can you use addition or multiplication to find the answer?
What estimation strategies might help you?

3–5 Measurement
What are the different parts of a shoe that you can measure? What tools and which units could you use to measure the different shoe parts?
What are some strategies for estimating measurements?

Vocabulary: length, width, height, volume, surface, area, pattern, texture, shape, color, estimate

Materials:

rulers, cubes, pencils, markers and/or colored pencils, 9-by-12-inch white construction paper, *All About My Shoe* recording sheets (see appendix and CD), scissors

Believe it or not, we conducted this activity with three classes combined, totaling around eighty students. To add to the challenge the grade levels were first, third, and fifth. We had the students sit at tables with a mix of grade levels, knowing the younger students would require more support and the older students would benefit from the opportunity to mentor their younger buddies. The students from Fay Elementary in San Diego visited the UC–San Diego campus and stopped by Caren's classroom for an hour to experience "a real college class." Knowing they'd all be wearing shoes, we took the opportunity to have them explore and investigate. Because we had a limited time frame, we barreled through a sequence of activities. You most likely will want to slow down and conduct these activities over several days. They're rich in both the mathematics and the visual arts connections.

To begin the lesson we asked the students how artists get their ideas. Because the grade range was vast and there were many English language learners in the group, we had them first talk briefly at their tables, both to generate ideas and to produce the language necessary to share with the whole group. When we asked the students to share some of the ideas that arose at their tables, they had a range of thoughtful responses:

Things that happen in their lives
How they express themselves
From other pictures
Their dreams
Their imagination
Museums
Using their five senses
Memories
School and learning about stuff

From the general discussion about artists' ideas we transitioned specifically to shoes. We asked the students to talk to a partner about what they noticed about their shoes. The goals for this partner talk were to help students notice the various features of their shoes and to produce the vocabulary they would need as the lesson progressed. As we conducted a brief whole-class discussion, we drew and labeled a shoe on the whiteboard. This visual reference gave students further access to the vocabulary.

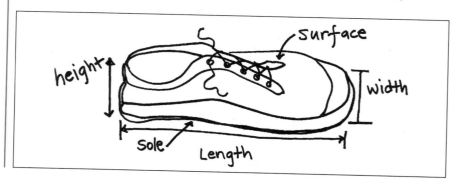

The next step was to show a brief slide show of different styles of shoes and different uses of shoes in art (such as shoe buildings, shoe cars, shoe chandeliers, and shoe bicycles). Students delighted in the shoe show. They oohed and aahed over every image. Something special happens when people see a common object presented in a unique and creative way. Students loved seeing shoes in contexts that weren't ordinarily "shoeish." Telling them it was their turn to be shoe artists, we let them know it was time for them to work on their own shoes.

"The first thing artists do is notice," we explained. "So we want you to notice and get to know your shoe in ways you probably haven't before. We have a recording sheet to help you keep track of all the things you learn about your shoe."

We showed them the *All About My Shoe* recording sheet and referred to the picture on the whiteboard to help them remember the names of the parts of the shoe and measurement terms.

The shoe exploration had three parts. First, the students estimated the measurements for different components of their shoes such as length, width, height, volume, surface area, and area of the sole. Then they did the actual measuring with the rulers and cubes we provided. (With older students and more time you can have students find the difference between the estimate and actual measurement.)

The next step involved students using their observation skills and vocabulary to describe their shoes. We prompted students to talk at their tables about the lines, shapes, colors, patterns, and textures they saw. They used their recording sheets to document what they noticed. We provided sentence frames on the recording sheet to assist the younger students and English language learners.

Finally students traced the sole of one of their shoes on a piece of 9-by-12-inch construction paper. They used this shoe outline to redesign their shoe, using some of the ideas presented earlier in the sequence. Markers and colored pencils gave students ways to create new patterns, shapes, and themes for their shoe design. These colorful, imaginative shoe shapes can be cut out and used for sorting, comparing, and graphing activities later. (See activities that follow.) They can also be posted along a wall as a border or used as nonverbal signage to mark a path.

The fact that first, third, and fifth graders all remained engaged and enthused throughout the activities speaks to the power of teaching mathematics through the visual arts. Some of the estimating and measuring activities served as practice for the older students, but it worked equally well as introduction and exposure for the younger ones. Plus, the younger students benefited from seeing older students as role models, and the older students reinforced their skills through teaching them to their younger tablemates. Certainly the shoe context and the hands-on approach to the activities allowed for all students to learn at their own level.

More *All About My Shoe* Activities

Students can do the following activities with the shoe cutouts they created in the initial activity just described or with their actual shoes. (They need to take off at least one shoe for most of these activities.)

Shoe Comparing

Grade Level:	K–2
Math Content Area:	Algebra
Math Overview:	*Shoe Comparing* gives students experience with identifying and describing attributes. They consider such mathematical features as size, shape, and weight. Use of descriptive and mathematical language develops students' abilities to communicate mathematically.
Guiding Questions:	What's the same about these shoes? How are these shoes different?
Vocabulary:	same, different, sort, color, pattern, line, shape, texture
Materials:	shoe cutouts or actual shoes

Elisabeth Frausto let us try the following two activities with her kindergartners. Have students sit on the rug in a circle or in some other configuration that allows for easy viewing of a set of objects. Take six to ten shoes and have students notice and describe their different components. Students may remark on the color, style, size, laces, or any number of details. Encourage them to use the vocabulary generated in the *All About My Shoe* lesson. Have them identify ways some shoes are the same and different. Pick two shoes to model as an example. Provide sentence frames: "These shoes are the same because they both have _____." "These shoes are different because one _____ and the other _____."

Partners can then go back to their seats with two shoes to compare. They can discuss the similarities and differences and record their ideas on a T-table.

SAME	DIFFERENT
Laces	one has black, one has no black
Line patterns	one is size 3, one is size 5
2 colors	one has a star, one has no stars
blue	one is a sandal, one is a sneaker
circles	the shapes are different
Dirty	

Shoe Sorting

Grade Level: K–2

Math Content Area: Algebra

Math Overview: *Shoe Sorting* allows students to group and classify shoes based on different attributes. This activity lays the groundwork for later algebraic thinking by having students seek patterns and consider and describe features and relationships.

Guiding Questions: How can we group these shoes so they fit different criteria?
How can we organize the shoes to show which criteria they fit?

Vocabulary: same, different, Venn diagram, circle, texture, shape, color

Materials: shoe cutouts or actual shoes, large piece of butcher paper with a large circle drawn on it slightly to one side

This activity builds on the *Shoe Comparing* experience. Have students sit in a circle with eight to ten shoes in the middle. Tell the students you are thinking of a secret category and are going to show them which shoes fit the category and which shoes don't. Their job is to guess the category. You might start with a simple category such as "has laces." As you sort the shoes, say to the students, "This shoe fits my secret category" and put it within the circle on the butcher paper or "This shoe doesn't fit my category" as you move the shoe onto the butcher paper outside the circle.

Encourage students to continue to use the vocabulary they've been using in the *All About My Shoe* lessons. Let students try to guess your secret category. If students are ready, they can generate their own categories, sort the shoes, and have the class try to guess their categories. You can also extend this activity by sorting shoes with a two-variable Venn diagram. Simply add another large overlapping circle to your butcher paper. Each circle represents a category (for example, "has laces," "has blue on it"), and shoes that fit both categories go in the middle of the two circles.

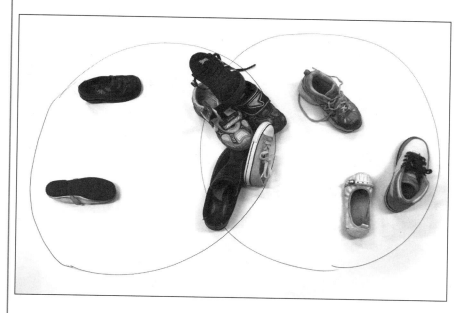

Shoe Graphing

Grade Level: K–2, 3–5

Math Content Area: Data Analysis and Probability

Math Overview: *Shoe Graphing* gives students an opportunity to organize data visually in a graph format. Students apply the vocabulary and concepts acquired through *Shoe Comparing* and *Shoe Sorting* to create shoe graphs that display shoes according to predetermined categories.

Guiding Questions:

K–2

Can we make a graph that tells how many shoes fit a certain category?

3–5

What questions can we ask about our shoes?

What types of graphs can help display information about the shoes in our classroom?

How can we use what we know about the shoes in our classroom to make predictions about shoes in other classrooms?

Vocabulary: graph, likely, unlikely, color, texture, pattern

Materials: shoe cutouts or actual shoes, butcher paper or graph paper, markers

This activity naturally extends from the *Shoe Sorting* activity. Once students proficiently identify different shoe attributes, they can create graphs to represent these attributes. Students can use Venn diagrams to represent overlapping attributes or bar graphs to represent singular features of a shoe. (How many lace holes does your shoe have? Does your shoe have stripes?)

Younger students benefit from seeing how data can be displayed in a variety of ways. Challenge older students to predict what the data might show in the class next door or even schoolwide: "It is likely that the shoes next door _____." "It is unlikely that the shoes next door _____." Older students can also collect and graph data about shoes in their classroom to hypothesize the features of "the average shoe" in their class.

LESSON | Masking Tape Shoes

Grade Level: 3–5

Math Content Areas: Geometry

Math Overview: Students grapple with key geometry concepts while creating masking tape shoes. They make mental images and consider an object from multiple perspectives. Students analyze the geometric properties of their shoes and break the three-dimensional shoe into two-dimensional components. From there they use the two-dimensional model to build a three-dimensional object.

Guiding Questions:
What are the different pieces of a shoe? Describe their shapes and relative size.
What new shapes do the pieces form when combined?
How do two-dimensional pieces combine to form a three-dimensional object?

Vocabulary: deconstruct, plan view, other views, visual weight, perspective, structure, construction, problem solving, two-dimensional, three-dimensional, plane

Materials: shoe, paper, pencil, one roll of masking tape per student, tools such as paper clips, pens, toothpicks

This activity really delivers. Kristin Komatsubara found great success with her intermediate-grade students. She started by having students view and sketch their shoes from a variety of perspectives: front, side, bird's-eye, and plan view. Then she had the students visually deconstruct their shoe, looking carefully at all its component parts. She prompted them by having them imagine a shoe factory. She asked students to think about the different pieces of the shoe that have to be put together. Then she had them do quick sketches of all the different parts of the shoe they could identify.

She pointed out that in these activities students represented a three-dimensional object (the shoe) on a two-dimensional plane (the paper).

Once students spent time thinking about the parts of the shoe and how shoes are put together, they were ready to construct their own shoe. The students' task was to make an actual-sized, detailed model of their shoe using only masking tape. Although it seemed impossible at first, Kristin reassured them of the viability of the project by showing some photos of other masking tape shoes. She pointed out that the successful tape shoes had "visual weight." Even though they consisted only of tape, they looked sturdy and seemed to have the weight of an actual shoe.

Kristin gave the students some time to hypothesize about and discuss the potential effectiveness of different techniques and tools. Then she brainstormed with students about possible approaches to the job. She gave them an opportunity to get started during class. She stopped them after ten or fifteen minutes to discuss how it was going, what was working, and how they planned to continue the work. Kristin gave them a due date for the final products. The students completed the project either at home or during independent work time. When the shoes were finished, the class had a gallery walk to appreciate each other's work. Afterward, Kristin displayed the tape shoes prominently outside her classroom. They impressed all who viewed them and represented a true problem-solving experience.

LESSON | Shoe Rubbings

Grade Level: 3–5

Math Content Area: Algebra

Math Overview: The *Shoe Rubbings* activity gives students multiple ways to represent algebraic data. From a concrete model, they find patterns and generate algebraic equations. They encounter geometric, graphic, and numeric representations of algebraic patterns.

Guiding Questions:
What patterns do you see?
How can the pattern be described with words, numbers, graphs, or equations?
Can you predict what the pattern would be on a larger shoe?

Vocabulary: line, diagonal, vertical, horizontal, perpendicular, angle, shape, intersection, pattern, texture, prediction, variable, repeating pattern, growth pattern, radial

Materials: shoe, crayons, *Shoe Rubbing* recording sheet (see appendix and CD)

This activity focuses on the patterns on the sole of the shoe. When we did it with Tina Rasori's fifth graders, we took a risk and hoped there would be enough variety and some tread patterns with algebraic implications. If you don't want to risk it, you might have each student bring in a shoe in advance so you can see what you're going to end up with. You need sole treads with either obvious repeating (e.g., square, triangle, square, triangle, etc.) or growth patterns (e.g., one square, two squares, three squares, etc.). If you're not thrilled with the selection, you can bring in one or two of your own shoes to make sure you have at least one example of a growth pattern on a shoe sole.

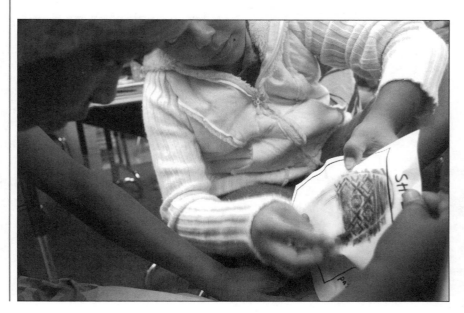

We began the session by telling students we were going to use an object that would connect math and art. We gave them three clues and told them to talk to a partner about what they thought this object might be.

It's something you wear.
It protects part of your body.
It goes over your sock.

It wasn't the most challenging riddle, but the students enjoyed the format and the opportunity to show how smart they were in solving the puzzle.

Because we knew the students were starting a unit on algebra, we mentioned how patterns play an important role in algebra. Then we asked the students to talk to a partner about patterns on their shoes. They generated a long list of words describing their shoes' patterns and attributes. We wrote the list on the board so students would have access to the vocabulary and ideas when they returned to their seats. The board was filled with words such as *bumpy, oval, square, line, hexagon, wavy, slanted, diamond,* and many more. This visual reference proved very helpful, especially for the many English language learners in the class.

We then pointed to the bottom of a sample shoe and told the class that we were focusing on the bottom or sole today. We modeled how to capture an impression of the sole with a crayon rubbing. To start we modeled capturing the imprint of the sole of my shoe by placing a piece of paper over it and rubbing across the paper with a crayon. The students knew the technique from detective and forensic TV shows, and it's the same technique that artist Robert Rauschenberg used.

After we got the rubbed image of the shoe sole, we reviewed relevant vocabulary and recorded it on the board for students' reference. We taped the shoe rubbing on the board and had students describe numbers and patterns that they noticed. Amazingly, Kevin immediately saw a number pattern (two rectangles, two rectangles, four rectangles, two, two, four . . .). The class generated a lot of words, which we added to the list on the board.

Then we gave the students a job. We posted the directions on the board since it was a multistep assignment:

Your Job
Work with a partner at your table.
Help each other make a shoe rubbing on your recording sheets.
Describe the shoe rubbing with words and numbers.
Tell about any patterns you notice.
Record your work on the *Shoe Rubbings* sheet.

Students went back to their tables to capture their own shoe rubbings and generate words, numbers, and patterns. They worked in pairs to capture a crayon imprint of the sole of their shoes on a *Shoe Rubbing* recording sheet. Students used math and art vocabulary to describe the patterns and shapes they saw on their shoe rubbings.

As the students worked, we circulated, checking on their progress and prompting them to record as much as possible on their papers. Our other

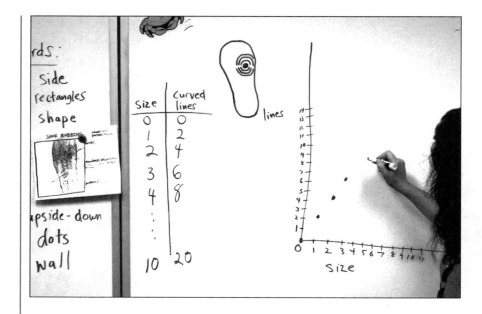

agenda item was to find a shoe pattern that could be modeled algebraically. Thankfully, we saw Katie's and realized the growth pattern of curved lines would fit nicely on a T-table and graph.

As mentioned earlier, we don't recommend this approach to finding an adequate shoe pattern; we just happened to luck out on this occasion. It's best to already have an example of a growth pattern before you start the lesson (find one of your own shoes or borrow someone's). You don't want the lesson to be dependent on luck, and it also helps to have the pattern in advance so you'll be prepared for the algebra that's generated.

We named the big circle in the middle Size 0 and then counted the curved lines above and below for each increasing size. Students saw patterns on the T-table and shared quite a few relationships they saw:

Take the size and add it to itself to get the number of curved lines.
Take the size and multiply by two to get the number of curved lines.
The sizes go up by ones.
The curved lines go up by twos.

Then we modeled graphing the data from the T-table. From the T-table and graph we challenged students to generate a formula that described the shoe pattern growth. We used letter variables to represent the size, number of lines, and curves. Students talked to a partner about how to describe the growth and how to condense that description into an algebraic equation. They had little trouble accomplishing this task, coming up with such equations as $S + S = C$, $2S = C$, $S = C / 2$.

The use of the shoe provided a relevant, visual model for students to use in both describing patterns and representing at least one of the patterns algebraically. The lesson proved a success and left rich possibilities for exploring other shoe growth patterns and describing them algebraically.

CHAPTER 7

THE FLAG

Flags fascinate children. Whether we're matching flags to home countries or waving pennants at a sports event, flags represent meaning, allegiance, and belonging. Thus, we saw the flag as an excellent object of focus. Students have prior experience with them, they're all around us, and they have inherent meaning.

Most classrooms have an American flag prominently displayed. They are symbols, icons, and have a story that's part of the history of the United States. Likewise, many world maps have legends or addendums that include flags of different countries.

We looked at flags as a way to connect mathematics, history, culture, geography, and visual art. Different types of flags serve different functions, and we wanted to share some existing flags as contexts for activities. We also wanted students to create their own flags with mathematical parameters and therefore work with design, mathematics, and visual arts to complete their projects.

We used different types of paper for most of the flag activities in this chapter. For activities that require a more authentic flag feel, we recommend

ACTIVITY	GRADES	NUMBER AND OPERATIONS	ALGEBRA	GEOMETRY	MEASUREMENT	DATA ANALYSIS AND PROBABILITY
Spin a Flag	K–2, 3–5			✓		✓
The Math Gates	K–2, 3–5	✓	✓	✓	✓	✓
Papel Picado	3–5	✓		✓		
Nautical Initial Flags	3–5			✓	✓	
Nautical Flag Fractions	3–5	✓				
Flag Variations	3–5	✓		✓		

felt, paper towel, or actual fabric. Inexpensive fabric can often be obtained by asking for the ends of fabric bolts. When there's not much fabric left, stores don't have a lot of options for it. They are frequently happy to discount or give the fabric away to a worthy educational cause.

THE FLAG AND THE MATHEMATICS

The makeup of flags—usually rectangular, comprising mostly regular shapes—provides math opportunities galore. Although we may have one mental image of a rectangular flag in our heads, flags actually come in a variety of rectangles. Some flags are close to squares, and others are longer, thinner rectangles. Helping students notice flags gives them a context for informally studying ratio and proportion. How do the lengths and widths of different-shaped flags compare? How does the ratio of length to width affect the shape of the rectangle?

Geometry, fractions, and measurement naturally arise from exploring the features of flags. The majority of the activities in this chapter focus on the natural connection between flags and geometric models of mathematical ideas. We also use flags as a context for exploring probability. Regardless of the math content area, flags provide an ideal way to bring a relevant visual context to core math concepts.

THE FLAG AND THE ART CONNECTIONS

Flags have served many purposes throughout history. Whether representing a country, an affiliation group, or an individual, flags are a symbol of identity and pride. Almost always a rectangle or triangle, flags or banners are seen in streets and buildings in every part of the world. Communities and villages use banners to designate territorial boundaries, announce an entryway, or guide travelers. Nautical flags are used on ships to communicate messages. Artists use flags both as subject and medium.

Flags provide a medium of communication for political messages. Because they are usually seen from a distance, printed on cloth, and are often waving, flags require the ability to be "read" quickly. The message or meaning of a flag is reduced to simple shapes and symbols of limited colors. The flag is a perfect object for problem solving for artists and mathematicians.

Many world cultures use flags to send a message, celebrate an event, or represent community. Tibetan Buddhists have a tradition of printing prayers on colored cloth to hang outside of sacred spaces and flutter in the wind, sending their spiritual messages out to the world. Historical paintings show flags and banners carried on foot and on horseback in battle scenes of Samurai warriors, medieval knights, and traditional village sporting events from around the world. It is hard to imagine a football, baseball, or basketball arena without team banners.

Noren are printed fabrics used in Japan. These rectangular banners are split in the middle and hung in doorways or between rooms to divide a space, designate an entry, or protect the opening to a room. Noren come in many different colors and sizes and are usually printed with patterns or traditional Japanese designs. Commercial shops use noren to display advertisements or the name of the store.

Papel picado, or "cut paper," is the traditional Mexican folk art of cutting rectangular pieces of brightly colored tissue paper. The rectangles are stacked up and the intricate images are chiseled through the whole stack at once. Stacks are then strung in rows of alternating colors and hung horizontally. Each papel picado is usually cut with designs from cultural celebrations such as Dia de los Muertos (Day of the Dead), an honoring of ancestors. Mexican communities also display them during other holidays and family celebrations.

Carmen Lomas Garza paints, writes children's books, creates installations, and makes paper cutouts. She works from the life events of her childhood growing up in south Texas. She created a series of paper cutouts based on traditional images from papel picado. In 1999 she was commissioned to create a large steel cutout for the San Francisco airport. Her book *Making Magic Windows: Creating Papel Picado/Cut-Paper Art with Carmen Lomas Garza* is a wonderful guide to teaching this traditional art form.

Christo and Jeanne-Claude have been collaborating artists since they met in 1958. Both were born on June 13, 1935. He is from Gabrovo, Bulgaria, and was named Christo Javacheff. She was born in Casablanca, Morocco, and named Jeanne-Claude Denat de Guillebon. They were married shortly after they met and use "Christo and Jeanne-Claude" as the name of their artist team. They moved to New York City in 1964. Jeanne-Claude died in 2009.

Christo and Jeanne-Claude have created monumental environmental projects. All of their projects are temporary installations made of fabric. They have used fabric to wrap the Reichstag building in Berlin, surround islands in Florida, and construct a fence in California that was 24.5 miles long and 18 feet high. Christo and Jeanne-Claude's work intentionally alters the environment and the viewers' experience. It is a temporary intervention into public space. In response to a question about why they had chosen to work that way, Jeanne-Claude responded, "The fact that the work does not remain creates an urgency to see it. For instance, if someone were to say, 'Oh, look on the right, there is a rainbow,' one would never answer, 'I will look at it tomorrow'" (http://christojeanneclaude.net).

They created projects so large and complex that it sometimes took decades for them to be approved for installation. Their planning process engaged municipalities, community members, engineers, politicians, and thousands of installers. All of their funding was generated through the sale of their original preparatory drawings. *The Gates*, a major project begun in 1979, was finally installed for sixteen days in New York City's Central Park in 2005. It included 7,503 16-foot-tall poles in the shapes of doorways with brightly colored saffron fabric flags hanging from each one.

Jasper Johns shocked the art world in the mid-1950s when he created the first of his series of paintings titled *Flag*. These paintings were made of encaustic (wax embedded with pigment) and look identical to the American flag. Taking an important cultural symbol, reproducing it, and changing its context generated much critique of what was considered art.

Johns was a prolific artist and experimented with many media. He greatly influenced the direction of Modern Art and became one of the most important icons of American art. What shocked the world even more was the record auction price of $28.6 million for the sale of *Flag* in May 2010.

Born in 1930 and still painting, Johns received the National Medal of Arts in 1990. He challenges us to ask questions and examine the meaning of objects and images. Does a flag remain a symbol if it becomes a flat painting? How much would you have to alter the shapes and colors of a familiar icon for it to lose its meaning? What is the artist's role in creating public discourse about society and culture?

The Flag and the Art Vocabulary: complementary colors, cool colors, encaustic, installations, medium, Modern Art, noren, papel picado, primary colors, print, secondary colors, warm colors

THE FLAG LESSONS

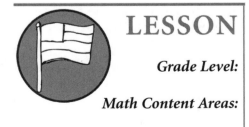

LESSON | Spin a Flag

Grade Level: K–2, 3–5

Math Content Areas: Geometry, Data Analysis and Probability

Math Overview: *Spin a Flag* gives students ways to make predictions and experience probability in the context of creating a flag. Younger students benefit from collecting data using concrete objects and describing and displaying that data. They also consider the likelihood of events. Older students compare different representations of the same data. They also predict the relative likelihood of events and conduct experiments to test their predictions. Students also explore ways shapes can be combined to create other shapes. Older students address symmetry and spatial reasoning as well.

Guiding Questions:

K–2
Geometry
    What shapes do you see?
    Can you find two shapes that combine to make a new shape?
Data Analysis and Probability
    What predictions can you make about what your flag might look like?
    Is it likely your flag will be all one color?
3–5
Geometry
    What is symmetry?
    How can you make your flag symmetrical?
Data Analysis and Probability
    What are some possible outcomes?
    What colors are more likely to appear on your flag? Why?
    What is an unlikely flag result? How do you know?

Vocabulary: prediction, likely, unlikely, equally likely, possible, impossible, data, certain, rectangle, triangle, square

Materials: crayons, polelike items (e.g., straws or dowels), tape, paper clips and pencils (to use on spinner), *Primary Colors Spinner* and blank *Flag Spinners* templates, flag templates, *Spin a Flag* recording sheet for level 3–5 (see appendix and CD)

Spin a Flag combines important ideas in probability with the designing of a flag. The activity is adaptable and can be used with any grade level. A primary version and an upper-grade version are described below.

Spin a Flag (K–2)

This activity focuses on making predictions and using math vocabulary as part of a probability experiment. The experiment results in unique flags that students create from the data generated in the experiment. To begin, show a rectangular flag template (Template 1) and ask students what they notice about it. They might share ideas about shapes, relative size of the shapes, and things the template reminds them of.

Next show the primary colors spinner and ask students to identify each section by its color. Ask students if they notice anything about the pieces of the spinner and help them connect the idea that the spinner is more likely to land on the larger pieces. Have them predict which color the paper clip will land on when you spin it. After the students make some predictions, spin the spinner, showing students how to use a pencil as the axis and a paper clip as the spinning part.

Model choosing one section of the flag template to color in with each spin. Then have the students predict again. Spin and color another section

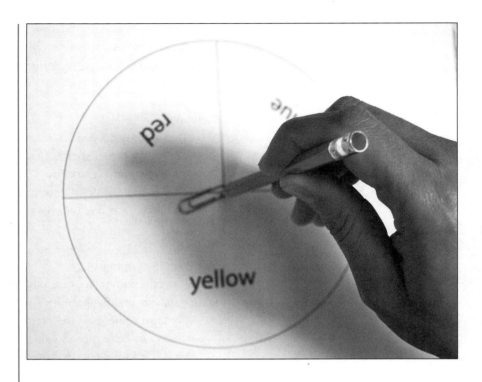

of the flag. Continue modeling until students have a clear understanding of the mechanics of the job.

Do one flag with the whole class. Give each student a copy of the flag template. Spin the spinner and have students decide which section of their flag they want to color that color. Having students point to the designated section or show a partner which section they plan to color with each spin helps them stay focused. Repeat the process until the students complete their flags. Wrap the end of the flag template around a straw, pencil, or dowel, and tape it so the flag is on a pole.

Display all the flags in the front of the room. Have students discuss their similarities and differences. Ask students why the flags look different even though everyone got their information from the same spinner and the same spins. Informally introduce probability vocabulary by asking students why none of the flags have any green on them. (There's no green on the spinner, so it's impossible.) Ask students why the flags aren't all red. (Although red is on the spinner, it's unlikely that every result will be red.)

To open up the investigation, allow students to choose their own spinner and flag template. Students can make some predictions verbally or in writing, depending on their grade level and writing abilities. Send students off in pairs to use their spinners and color their flag templates. Having partners helps with the spinning. One student can hold the pencil and paper clip in the middle of the spinner while the other partner flicks the paper clip to make it spin. As a follow-up activity, students can try to match different flags to the spinners they think generated them. Inserting the bottoms of the flagpoles into small lumps of modeling clay makes the flags freestanding and easier to display on a tabletop or chalk tray.

Spin a Flag (3–5)

The introduction to this activity can be very similar to the primary version. Show the basic spinner and ask students what they notice about it. Ask them which colors are more likely to be landed on, less likely, and impossible. Then model spinning and recording the results on a flag template.

The intermediate flag templates (Templates 2 and 3) possess mirror images so that when the flag is complete and mounted on a pole (straw) it will look the same on both sides. This requires students to color two sections after each spin—the section of their choice and its mirror image on the opposite side of the template. This part of the task poses challenges for some students, so a brief discussion and modeling before independent work helps. (It's actually not a big deal if both sides don't look exactly alike, but it's good for the students to at least try this spatial challenge.)

After students have the basic idea of how to spin and how to design the double-sided flag, have them choose a flag template and a spinner to use. Tell them to discuss and make some predictions about the results they imagine. When students finish their flags, have them show them to their tablemates.

Distribute the *Spin a Flag* recording sheet and have them complete items 1 and 2. After they have completed their flags, they can finish the recording sheet. The recording sheet helps the students focus on the probability ideas and forces them to use important concepts and vocabulary. For example, one student wrote, "I was surprised about landing on blue so many times even though it was only ¼ of the circle." Another observed, "If there are larger fractions of a color on the spinner, the probability of landing on that color is greater."

Students can also create their own spinners using the blank *Flag Spinners* template. They can extend the flag designs by adding more personal elements to the flag sections, rather than just coloring the flag in. For example, students might create spinners with sections directing them to fill in flag sections with the following:

Something you're good at
An important person in your family
A food you like
A special place you like to visit
A dream you have

Brainstorming a list of ideas to choose from provides students with ideas and language they can access when designing their spinners.

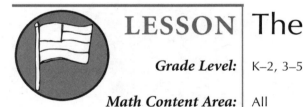

LESSON | The Math Gates

Grade Level:	K–2, 3–5
Math Content Area:	All
Math Overview:	This activity engages students in considering important elements of mathematics and displaying them visually. Because the activity is open-ended, it provides teachers with an excellent assessment opportunity. Students can express their ideas about mathematics and its key components. They communicate what they understand and value about mathematics.
Guiding Questions:	What are some important patterns we use in math? What are some important words we use in math? What are some important symbols we use in math? What are some important geometric shapes we use in math?
Vocabulary:	symbol, pattern, shape, geometry
Materials:	sketch paper, nylon, banner material, or felt (all one color with no pattern); permanent markers or crayon; scrap material; staples; glue stick, glue gun, or needle and thread; dowel or string; hammer and nails or duct tape

Inspired by Christo and Jeanne-Claude's project called *The Gates*, installed in New York City, students create "math gates" for installation in their school. Start by introducing *The Gates* to the students and showing them some images (see the CD that accompanies this book for a sample math gate). Emphasize how Christo and Jeanne-Claude desired to temporarily transform an environment through their art installation. Also show some images of Japanese noren and ask students to compare them with *The Gates*.

Tell the students they are going to undertake a similar, smaller project to create math gates for their school. These math gates will be installed in the doors down one hallway of the school. The effect will be similar to a series of hanging noren.

Give each student a 12-by-18-inch piece of fabric. Have them measure a 2-inch margin at the top of the long end and mark it off. This area needs to be reserved for installation. When completed, the top part will be folded around a thin rope and stapled. The result will be three 12-by-16-inch fabric gates hanging above each door, leaving enough room to walk underneath.

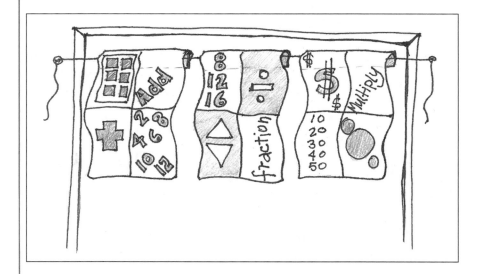

Next ask students to talk in groups about important ideas in math. Specifically tell them to think about math symbols, math vocabulary, math patterns, and math shapes. Write *Symbols, Words, Patterns,* and *Shapes* on the board as headings. Have students brainstorm in their groups about math words and ideas that fit under each heading. After a few minutes call the students back to share their ideas with the whole class. As students share their thinking, record their contributions on the board. Results may include the following ideas.

Symbols	Words	Patterns	Shapes
+	add	odd #s	triangle
−	multiply	even #s	square
=	divide	multiples	rectangle
x	subtract	square #s	pentagon
/	fraction		hexagon
%	equivalent		trapezoid
$	times		circle

Prompt students to consider what images might represent some of the words listed on the board. For example, they might represent even numbers as pairs of circles or other items. After discussing and modeling a few drawings on the board, ask students to choose one item from each of the four categories and then use paper and pencil to sketch images that represent each item. As a challenge, ask students to find ways to connect the four images. Once they have sketched out their images, they transfer them onto their fabric swatch. Give students the option of using markers, crayons, felt, and glue to design their "gate." Remind them to leave the top margin of their fabric free for the installation later.

The open-ended nature of the task ensures a variety of approaches and final products. Wrap and staple the short sides of three gates to a rope long enough to leave about 6 inches extending past a doorway on either side. Secure the rope to nails that are placed just above and to the sides of the doorjamb, making sure the gates are hung on the door so that it can open without obstruction. Attaching the rope to the doorjamb with duct tape will also work.

When the gates are hung, students will marvel at the effect on the school. They truly create a Christo-and-Jeanne-Claude-like effect on their environment. Walking through the math gates celebrates mathematics and transforms the hallways and entryways into a mathematical wonderland. This activity can be done with larger rectangles and strung across the hallways to even greater effect.

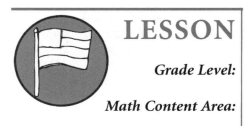

LESSON

Papel Picado

Grade Level: 3–5

Math Content Area: Number and Operations, Geometry

Math Overview: Creating a papel picado requires students to consider number patterns such as doubling and exponential growth. Students also consider fractions as they investigate positive and negative space on each papel picado. The activity challenges students to visualize shapes and their locations on a plane. Further geometric and spatial thinking involves predicting what types of shapes result from cutting folded paper and then unfolding it.

Guiding Questions:

Number and Operations

When you unfold your paper, how much bigger will the new shapes be compared with the shapes you originally cut?

What fraction is positive space?

What fraction is negative space?

Geometry

Can you predict the shape you'll have when you unfold your paper?

Where are the lines of symmetry?

How can you create shapes in specific parts of your papel picado?

Vocabulary: symmetry, positive space, negative space, complementary colors, warm colors, cool colors, primary colors

Materials: sheets of 9-by-12-inch tissue paper, small sharp scissors, construction paper, glue, color wheel

Papel picado means "perforated paper" in Spanish. This Mexican folk art traditionally celebrates special occasions such as weddings and holidays. Certain colors are usually associated with certain holidays (for example, pink, orange, and purple for Dia de los Muertas, or Day of the Dead; and red, white, and green for Mexican national holidays).

We used this activity to help students consider color relationships as well as mathematics. To start we asked students to choose two colors. One of the colors would be for the tissue paper papel picado, and the other would serve as the construction paper background for the finished product. We reviewed categories of colors by writing the headings on the board: *Cool, Warm, Primary, Secondary,* and *Complementary.* Referring to a color wheel helps students who are unfamiliar with primary, secondary, and complementary colors.

We listed colors that fall under each category.

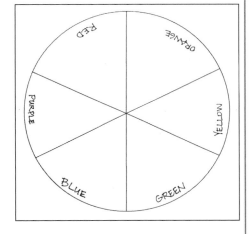

Cool	Warm	Primary	Secondary	Complementary
blue	red	red	purple	yellow and purple
green	orange	yellow	orange	orange and blue
purple	yellow	blue	green	green and red

Students began with their tissue paper. They folded the paper into fourths (edge to edge, not diagonally). Students could either fold the paper once in one direction and then in the other direction to make four rectangular boxes, or they could do an accordion fold resulting in four long, thin rectangles. Without unfolding, students began to cut shapes through parts of

the folded paper. We reminded students that it didn't matter which edges they cut as long as the paper stayed intact. When students unfolded their paper, they delighted in their results.

We had students share their work with a partner and identify lines of symmetry. We also asked them to talk with their partners about the relationships between the shapes they cut out and the shapes that emerged when they unfolded their paper. These discussions reinforced geometric vocabulary (names of shapes) and helped students use their spatial reasoning to visualize the component pieces combining to create the unfolded final shape. As students shared their papel picado, we offered a challenge. We told them to pair up and try to re-create their partner's design. We prompted them to think about how the original paper was folded and where the cuts were made. They also needed to consider the shape of the cutouts. This part of the activity proved both engaging and challenging. Students stretched their spatial reasoning and visualizing skills to guess how their partners created each papel picado.

We could have ended the activity at this point and hung the papel picado on a string stretched across the room. However, we wanted to push for more math and art, so we had students mount their papel picado on the piece of construction paper they had chosen earlier. We gave them a few minutes to notice the color contrasts and connect them to the color categories we had discussed earlier. Then we had students consider the positive and negative space of their papel picado. The color contrast made it easier to see the negative space because it was highlighted by the construction paper background. We asked the students to estimate fractions to describe the positive and negative space of their papel picado. Having students justify their estimates (verbally or in writing) further reinforces their mathematical thinking and communication.

LESSON

Grade Level:

Math Content Areas:

Math Overview:

Guiding Questions:

Nautical Initial Flags

3–5

Geometry, Measurement

Nautical Initial Flags present a context for exploring shape, scale, and measurement strategies. Students break shapes on a plane into smaller shapes and areas to produce enlarged models. Issues of perspective, pattern, and problem solving arise from the work.

Geometry
   What shapes do you see in the flag?
   Can you see smaller shapes and patterns that make up your flag design?
Measurement
   What measurement tools can you use to create an initial flag?
   What are some different ways to measure?
   What parts of the flag can you measure to help you with your job?

Vocabulary: parallel lines, right angle, acute angle, obtuse angle, similar, rectangle, square, fractions

Materials: rulers, 3-inch white construction paper squares, colored pencils, *Nautical Flag Chart* (see CD), tape, straws or other polelike materials for mounting flags

"Raise your hand if you've seen a boat," we said to fourth and fifth graders in Yen Dang's and Elizabeth McEvoy's classes. Everyone raised a hand. We decided to start with a simple prompt that tapped into the students' prior knowledge. From there we asked students to talk at their tables and name different things they'd seen on boats. They quickly began animated discussions. We overheard a group mention flags, so we seized on that as an entry into our activity. If we hadn't heard someone mention flags, we would have let students share a few of their ideas and then brought up flags ourselves. We pointed out that boats have flags and those flags actually mean special things: "Here's a hint. *Nautical* means something that has to do with boats or sailors. There are twenty-six different square nautical flags. Can you think of any reason why there are twenty-six different nautical flags? Do you know anything else that comes in a group of twenty-six?"

Many hands flew into the air. The range of guesses to what we supposed was an obvious question was surprising and refreshing.

"Different countries?" offered one student.

"Maybe there are twenty-six parts of a boat," suggested another.

We decided to give a hint—a really big hint. We pointed at the alphabet posted above the board in the front of the room.

"That's right," Lynn acknowledged. "There are twenty-six nautical flags because there are twenty-six letters in the alphabet. Each nautical flag represents a different letter. Each flag also represents a signal so boats can communicate with other boats. For example, the flag that means C also means 'yes.' The flag that represents *D* also means 'keep clear' or 'stay away.'"

We projected an image of the nautical flags in front of the room (see flag images on the accompanying CD). Students oohed and aahed. We pointed out that all nautical flags use only certain colors (red, blue, white, yellow, and black) because they are the most visible colors at sea. Also, the flags use only certain color combinations because they can be seen best from far away. We gave the students a few moments to look at the flags. Then we asked for a volunteer, picked a student, and wrote her name on the board. We asked the students what this girl's initials were.

Because there were many English language learners in the room, it was important to use and model the vocabulary in context before sending the students off for independent work. We underlined our volunteer's first and last initial and then asked students to find the two corresponding nautical flags. To reinforce this idea we told the students to turn to a partner and tell what their initials were. Then they needed to match their initials to the corresponding nautical flags. After they identified them, we explained that they were going to make their own nautical initial flags. We showed the half page of nautical flags reference sheet with all the flags and their corresponding letters. We also held up a sample 3-inch square.

"You're going to find your nautical initials on the small paper and copy them each on a square. This will be challenging for a few reasons," Lynn explained. "First, the paper square you're getting is bigger than the picture of the flag, but you want them to look the same. You need to figure out how to make a similar design on a larger square. The other big challenge is trying to make your flag look the same on both sides. When boats fly their flags, they need to look the same from all angles. That way if another boat approaches them, the people on that boat will be able to see the flag whether they're coming from the front or the back or the sides. The flags tell important messages so they need to be read from any angle."

We told students to talk at their tables about things they might do or ways they might approach the job that would help them address these challenges. We wrote their ideas on the board:

Use Geometry	**Use Fractions**
Shape	Fold the paper in half.
Angles	Use a ruler to measure and mark.
Parallel lines	Estimate.
Perpendicular lines	

We pointed to the *H* flag and asked students how they might copy that one onto a larger square. Many of them mentioned folding the square in half or using a ruler. We focused on a few other fairly easy flag designs (*E, L, N, O*) and had students talk to partners about how they might re-create those designs. Then we moved to a few of the more challenging designs (*I, P, V, S*) and had students pick one and think about what approach they'd use to copy that flag onto a square. We asked them to talk to a partner about their ideas. These brief discussions helped prepare them for the independent work to come.

When we felt confident that the students understood their job and had enough tools to tackle it, we let them get to work. We distributed half-page color reference sheets (included on the accompanying CD) with pictures of the nautical flags and their corresponding letters. We also made sure students had rulers and pencils at their tables so they could sketch out the designs of their flags on their paper squares before coloring them in. We circulated as the students worked, observing, listening, and asking questions. The students' different approaches intrigued us.

Gilberto needed to divide his first initial flag into six equal horizontal stripes. He approached the task by using a ruler and dividing each half of the flag into three stripes. As he explained, "After I did one half, I skipped eight little lines [on the ruler] and made a line and skipped another eight and drew a line. Now I'm done with the right side. Then I went to the left side and did the same thing. I ended up with six stripes."

Nadine began with a completely visual approach to her *N*. She first attempted to draw the checkerboard pattern freehandedly. Between the pattern and the colors it was difficult for her to see that the flag pattern was just sixteen equal squares within the large square. Instead she focused on the stair-step pattern of the tops of the blue squares. This focus made it difficult for her to accurately duplicate the pattern. She didn't recognize the straight horizontal and vertical lines until we used a ruler to show her. With some prompting she moved to a folding approach and then easily colored in every other square to create her design.

Students worked diligently on their flags. In addition to the engaging mathematical challenges, they were excited about the flags, and personalizing the activity through the use of their initials added to the investment. We often had to remind them to consider both sides of their flags and make sure they looked the same. Fortunately we had plenty of extra squares and could encourage students to try again if their initial attempt didn't match the model.

When students finished their two initials, we offered them the option of doing their middle initial or doing the initials of a family member. These extensions allowed flexibility within the construct of a whole-class lesson. As students got close to completing their initial flags, we stopped them to model how to attach their flags to a flagpole. This part of the job was quite simple. We just modeled attaching two tape tabs to the square and wrapping it around the pole.

To close the activity we had students share their flags with other students at their table. Then we picked a few flags to show to the whole class. We played a guessing game in which students had to guess whose flags they might be. We also showed the nautical flags and the messages they represented. We asked students to decipher what their nautical initial flags might signal. This part of the lesson could easily turn into a creative writing activity.

LESSON

Nautical Flag Fractions

Grade Level: 3–5

Math Content Area: Number and Operations

Math Overview: Students use nautical flags to explore an area model of fractions and fractional pieces. They use both estimation and computations to calculate the fractional parts each color on the flag represents. Because the pieces are not always adjacent, students visually manipulate and combine pieces to consider their fractional amounts.

Guiding Questions:
What fractions do you see on your flag?
How can you tell what fraction each color is?
What strategies can you use to figure out the fractions?

Vocabulary: fraction, half, quarter, whole, estimate, area

Materials: *Nautical Initial Flag* recording sheet (see appendix and CD), nautical initial flags (from prior activity)

We followed up the *Nautical Initial Flags* activity with Yen Dang and Elizabeth McEvoy's classes, this time focusing on fractions. Students looked at their initial flags to determine the fractional parts of each color. We provided a recording sheet that focused specifically on connecting their flag work to important ideas about fractions.

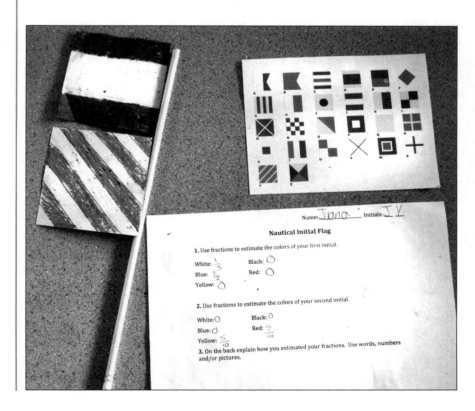

Both teachers we worked with thought the activity was rich and rewarding. As Elizabeth noted, "It's really good because it makes them think about what the fractions mean. It helps them think beyond just steps and procedures."

Yen also saw great value in the activity. As she explained, "There's so much potential for revisiting this activity." In fact, Yen followed up the experience by creating a series of questions for her students. She had them discuss the questions and then write and explain some of their answers. Yen's questions are listed below.

1. What do you think of each flag? Which looks hardest to copy? Why? Which looks easiest to copy? Why?
2. How do these flags make you think of math?
3. Order the flags in difficulty from easiest to hardest.
4. Identify all the flags with blue and estimate what percent of each flag is blue.
5. Identify all the flags with yellow and estimate what percent of each flag is yellow.
6. Identify all the flags that show one-half. Pick one to explain how you know it's one-half.
7. Identify all the flags that show one-fourth. Pick one to explain how you know it's one-fourth.
8. Identify all the flags that show one-eighth. Pick one to explain how you know it's one-eighth.
9. Identify all the flags that show one-third. Pick one to explain how you know it's one-third.
10. Identify all the flags that show one-sixth. Pick one to explain how you know it's one-sixth.
11. What did you learn from this lesson?

Yen also thought about modifications and extensions for the *Nautical Initial Flags* activity. Below are her ideas for teaching a nautical flag sequence in the future.

Lesson 1:

As a class, draw/make these flags while emphasizing the geometry (right angles, parallel lines, rectangles, squares, and so on).

Lesson 2:

Have students work together to discuss, compare, and arrange the flags by levels of difficulty while somehow encouraging them to use simple fractions to guide their thinking. Guide the students to start with bigger fractions. For example, it's easy to cut a flag into halves and fourths and not so easy to cut it into eighths or twelfths.

Lesson 3:

Make a big class set of these flags to put on the wall. These flags could be made again and again, and students may even alter the colors. The making of a big class set of nautical flags (10-by-10-inch size) would be nice to put up on the walls to be used as a reference when teaching fractions and percents. The teacher could have students refer to these pictures when they have trouble remembering how to draw fractions or need to think about various percents, very much the way students use the multiplication table.

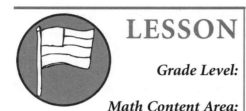

LESSON | Flag Variations

Grade Level: 3–5

Math Content Area: Number and Operations, Geometry

Math Overview: By analyzing and redesigning flags, students deepen their understanding of fractions as parts of wholes and the area model of fractions. Students use benchmarks and equivalent fractions to help them with their work. Focusing on actual flags gives students relevant, real-world contexts for estimating and computing with fractions.

Guiding Questions:
Number and Operations
Can you estimate a fraction for each color on the flag? How did you do it?
Would rearranging the colors help you estimate or combine the pieces?
Geometry
What shapes do you see within the flag?
Can you use the shapes to help estimate fractions?
Can you find any similar pieces that can help with your estimates?

Vocabulary: estimate, fraction, part, whole, area, equivalent, benchmark

Materials: sample flags from different countries, colored construction paper, 9-by-12-inch black or white construction paper for background, rulers, scissors, glue, flag pictures (see CD)

Jasper Johns inspired this activity. The main task is to analyze a flag in terms of its fractional parts and create several new flag designs by varying the colors and layout. This activity provides for differentiated instruction, because students can choose (or teachers can assign) flags at various degrees of difficulty. Following are some flag suggestions at different levels:

Easy flags: Armenia, Indonesia, France, Italy
Moderate: Latvia, Benin, Japan, Algeria, Mexico
Difficult: Macedonia, United States, Jamaica, Botswana

Start the lesson by introducing Jasper Johns and his fascination with the American flag. Show some of his flag work. Next model how to re-create the Indonesian flag from red and white construction paper. Ask students to identify the colors of the flag and the fraction of the flag that each color covers. Cut and glue red and white construction paper onto a background

sheet to create an Indonesian flag. Have students choose two new colors to replace the red and white and use them to create an alternative version of the Indonesian flag à la Jasper Johns. Finally, go back to the original flag and ask how you might design a new flag that's half red and half white but doesn't look like Indonesia's. Students will come up with a variety of ideas and designs. Choose one to model in front of the class so they can see the process.

Depending on students' comfort level, do a slightly more challenging flag with the whole class or allow individuals to pick a flag and redesign it, first using new colors and then rearranging the original colors in a new design. Then have students choose a flag to study and explore. Have them create three construction paper versions of the flag: the original flag, the original flag design with different colors, and a new flag with the same colors and proportions but in a different configuration. These types of artistic explorations are a way for students to think about creating unique aesthetic solutions to variations of the same problem. They are open-ended enough to stimulate creative thinking while building on basic design elements.

CHAPTER 8

THE JOURNAL

Journals play a key role in documenting an individual's ideas and growth. People keep all types of journals—writing journals, dream journals, art journals, diaries, math journals. They serve a multitude of purposes, including documenting, planning, and reflecting. A journal is a common object with uncommon potential. Both artists and mathematicians frequently keep journals.

There's something special about a journal specifically dedicated to one topic or endeavor. Although the activities described in this chapter could be done separately on individual sheets of paper, the cumulative effect of a bound group of pages enhances the overall project and the tasks embedded within.

We'd like to offer some ways to help teachers creatively integrate math and visual art. This chapter outlines some important ideas about math/art journals and also describes specific prompts and activities. We attempt to give a context for math/art journal usage and encourage teachers to develop a plan that best fits the needs and focus of their classrooms. These journal activities and prompts span the grade levels and math content areas. We encourage teachers (and their students) to be creative with the uses of their math/art journals. In fact, we found that by asking students to brainstorm ideas, the journals became both more inventive than we might have imagined and more personal, since the ideas came from the students themselves.

We'd also like to make a pitch for teachers keeping journals along with their students—writing in their own journals during writing time or reading a book during silent reading time. If teachers take the time to engage in some of the math/art journal activities in front of their students, they are sending a clear message about the importance and value of the work. Also, students and teachers benefit from the community that is developed through sharing journal work.

THE JOURNAL AND THE MATHEMATICS

Many teachers ask their students to keep math journals. Often, students start math class with a problem of the day or math practice question they complete in their math journal. The math journal provides an open format for students to organize and express their mathematical ideas and understanding. The chronological nature of the journal also gives teachers and students an opportunity to reflect on and assess growth and progress. The mathematical potential of a journal is as open-ended as its blank pages are. Virtually any math content area and almost any type of prompt can be addressed in a math journal. The most effective journal activities allow individual students to express their unique ways of thinking and solving problems.

THE JOURNAL AND THE ART CONNECTIONS

Artists use sketchbooks or journals to work out and record their ideas, sketch designs for larger projects, and practice daily drawing. Students can keep individual journals specific to an object as well as general ongoing art and math journals. Designing and creating personalized journals is a great way to introduce art at the beginning of the school year. Art journals are a personal visual diary in which students can practice drawing techniques, invent a personalized symbol system, and reflect on classroom activities in visual language. Some students really take to the daily journaling process and fill up many journals throughout the school year. The activities in this chapter are much like what adult art students and professional artists engage in. Journals provide an important portfolio record of the learning process. Almost all artists keep journals and portfolios to document and represent their significant work.

An art journal is one object common to almost every artist. If you google "art journal" images, you will find literally thousands of pages of artists' work. There are art journal blogs, digital sketchbooks, and journals that art groups share and contribute to collectively. There are also beautifully printed publications of artists' personal journals. Artists use many of the new social networking sites as a virtual public forum to share journal entries and images. Online publishing sites allow people to share their own visual journals. But nothing compares with the intimacy and simplicity of pencil on paper.

Students of all ages should be encouraged to draw regularly. A daily routine of five to ten minutes of drawing time is an important part of each day. Drawing time can consist of open-ended exploration or short exercises designed to stretch student thinking. It is important to remind students that everyone can draw, that drawing is a mode of communication, and that their drawings are personal and won't be judged by others. Drawing skill develops through concentrated practice. Students will use this skill throughout their lives as artists, mathematicians, scientists, problem-solvers, and communicators.

Daily drawing has many rewards. It is a time to explore ideas, brainstorm solutions, practice technique, and develop new learning strategies. It can be a contemplative time, a social time, or a transition time to help refocus between activities. Switching modalities from auditory to visual provides a different perspective for creative problem solving. Understanding visual symbol systems and competency in communicating in visual language plays an important role for students of math and art. Everyone has an internalized visual vocabulary, a library of images that helps us decode the world. Developing drawing skills can help us to understand and communicate our experiences and ideas. The ability to visualize information enhances and supports learning in all areas of the curriculum.

Children's artistic development includes a specific phase in which they want to depict an object accurately and realistically. Art educators have observed a concrete (and sometimes frustrating) period that students enter somewhere between the third and fifth grades. Students can be judgmental and self-critical during this phase. We often hear in a classroom, "He's the best artist in the class—he can draw things so real." This comment suggests that being a good artist is dependent upon one's ability to create accurate representational drawings. Journals offer the prospect of shifting the dialogue to "She came up with a really unique solution" or "I've never seen a drawing like that before; how did you get the idea?" Comments such as those remind students that the artist's ideas and unique solutions are most important. Supportive, nonjudgmental environments help students develop creativity, loosening restrictive views of what art can be and stretching their imaginations. Many students delight in the freedom from needing to create realistic drawings and enjoy engaging in imaginative journal drawing.

The daily journal activities connect well to contemporary art practices. The journal itself is considered both an art form and an important art process. Process Art describes an artistic style or movement that resonates with these activities. Process Art emphasizes the activity rather than its product. Process artist Jackson Pollock was famous for introducing "action painting." This technique involved dripping and splattering paint onto a canvas on the floor. Pollock focused on the internal process that occurred while he engaged in making art, much like the journaling process. His paintings were very abstract and made without using a paintbrush. Many questioned whether his work could even be called painting. He helped change some of the conventions of what was considered art in the 1940s and '50s. His work is considered to be an important early experiment in Process Art.

Danica Phelps records the many different daily activities of her life in a journal. Her artwork is made up of the visual display of the data collected in her daily calendar. She has tracked every dollar spent and earned, recorded every meal out, and clocked the time spent walking her dog. (Note: not all the information and images displayed in her work are appropriate for children.) She has created long chronological wall-sized line drawings and elaborate color-coded charts and graphs from her daily journal entries. It may be hard to imagine someone creating interesting art from such mundane statistical information, but her artwork transforms the activities of daily life into something visually compelling and engaging, if somewhat absurd.

Journals can serve as a starting point for many larger projects and pieces. Sketches, ideas, and measurements begun in journals can turn into monumental art pieces. Claes Oldenburg and Coosje van Bruggen, a husband-and-wife art team, create sculptures that dramatically change the scale and material of a familiar object. They are best known for their huge replicas of everyday objects found in public plazas, such as a 45-foot-tall steel clothespin, a 96-foot-tall baseball bat, a monumental lipstick tube, and a series of giant thumbtacks large enough to stand under. Oldenburg's early "soft sculptures" made from fabric are collected in museums worldwide. Both artists also exhibit their drawings and prints that represent a single object in monumental scale. Children naturally love this art, which seems to create fanciful characters from inanimate objects. Their work is a whimsical and delightful experience that shifts our thinking about the objects and the world around us. Students benefit from exposure to the process of beginning with ideas and sketches in a journal and translating those initial ideas into larger, more refined finished products.

The Journal and the Art Vocabulary: action painting, collage, contour, portfolio, Process Art

JOURNAL TYPES

There are many types of journals and many formats that work well for the math/art journal project. Some schools provide composition books that can be used as journals. If resources are available for purchasing journals, we recommend spiral-bound, hardcover journals smaller than 8½ by 11 inches. Having a journal that's a different size than standard school paper makes it special. Spiral binding allows any part of the journal to be opened

360 degrees, making it conveniently half the size. The hard cover gives it an added level of legitimacy and durability. All that being said, some teachers we worked with cut up drawing paper, stapled it together, and had students decorate the cover. Those journals worked just fine too. We do recommend tagboard or construction paper over newsprint or copy paper. It's best for a journal page to be able to handle media such as paint, markers, or glue.

GETTING THE OBJECT JOURNALS STARTED

We had students focus their math/art journal work on specific objects, either toothbrushes or walnuts. We gave one group of students daily toothbrush prompts to do at home. After the first week students brought in their journals to share with the class. We also did some in-class follow-up activities with the students, using class time to expand upon some of the activities they had done in their journals. For example, the students drew half-sized toothbrushes in their journals. Then in class we asked them to make a half-sized toothbrush and a three-times-enlarged toothbrush from clay. Connecting this activity to the work of Oldenburg and van Bruggen strengthens the art connection.

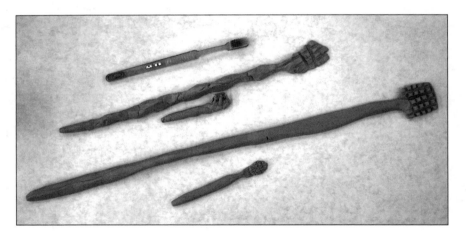

We also used class time to brainstorm other toothbrush journal activities for them to try at home the next week.

The walnuts also worked well. We gave a walnut to each student on the day we introduced the journal project. We asked the students to keep the walnuts with them for two weeks. We wanted them to get to "know their nut" intimately. Within a week the walnuts, which began as indistinguishable members of a nut colony, became recognizable individuals with readily describable attributes and characteristics.

Students could literally pick their nut out of a lineup. We had groups of four to six students put their walnuts in a brown paper lunch bag. Then they spilled the mixed nuts onto their table and tried to find their own. This activity, which would have been nearly impossible on the first day, was a complete no-brainer within the week. Students knew their nuts so well that they could easily distinguish their walnut from a group of walnuts. The students even expressed confidence in their ability to find their walnut from among the whole class collection. Learning to "see" is the artist's most fundamental task. In *Ways of Seeing* John Berger reminds us, "Seeing comes before words. The child looks and recognizes before it can speak . . . It is seeing which establishes our place in the surrounding world" (1972, 7). A considered and thoughtful approach to seeing applies to all art activities. Similarly, students who see patterns, relationships, details, and connections in mathematics more readily succeed in their problem-solving endeavors. Encouraging students to stop, look, notice, and think develops their habits of mind. The math/art journal activities provide an open forum for these processes.

Again, we encourage teachers to do the journal activities they assign to their students. When teachers keep their own journals, the journal activities become even more significant. This parallel work helps validate the interest and importance of the work. Math/art journals provide a place where students can feel that their own work is equal in value to the work of adults. It also gives the teacher insight into the creative process and a firsthand view of how visual art and mathematics work together.

We found that in order to encourage students' openness to various prompts and assignments it was important to start with a very nonthreatening assignment that would not rely on their abilities to accurately copy the object. For one class we started by having students do a blind contour drawing of their toothbrush. We modeled the *Blind Contour Portraits* activity (see Chapter 1, "The Face") in class and had students pair up and do blind contour portraits of each other. With this experience under their belt they had the skills and understanding to undertake their toothbrush blind contour journal assignment. For the walnut group's initial prompt, we asked students to draw their walnut with their nondominant hand. Both introductory assignments forced the students to really look at their objects while producing funny, less-than-lifelike drawings.

OBJECT JOURNAL PROMPTS

Following is a list of potential journal prompts we used for the toothbrush journals. The vast majority of prompts work well for the walnut too. Some prompts feature more of an art focus, some more math, and some clearly combine the two. We give credit to the students for generating many of these ideas.

We offer these prompts as possible assignments for your students. We encourage you to consider your math and art goals and choose prompts that best meet your objectives. Giving students some choice about which activities they do further personalizes the journals. Also, allowing students to generate some journal prompts promotes creativity and affirms their ability to take charge of their own learning.

> Draw your toothbrush with your nondominant hand.
> Do a blind contour drawing of your toothbrush.
> Draw your toothbrush with a burnt stick (parental supervision required).
> Draw your toothbrush in an outdoor environment.

Draw your toothbrush in a social setting with other toothbrushes.

Draw six different views of your toothbrush on the same page.

Use toothpaste to finger-paint your toothbrush.

Draw a greatly enlarged part of your toothbrush.

Draw cross sections of your toothbrush every ¼ inch.

Draw your toothbrush with your toothbrush.

Draw your toothbrush continuously for ten minutes.

Make a toothbrush pattern drawing.

Draw yourself brushing your teeth.

Draw the negative space around your toothbrush.

Draw your toothbrush brushing your top teeth.

Draw your toothbrush brushing your bottom teeth.

Draw your toothbrush brushing your tongue.

Show your toothbrush rinsing under the faucet.

Draw your toothbrush made only of triangles.

Draw your toothbrush made only of rectangles.

Draw your toothbrush made only of circles.

Use a pencil to show the different shades of your toothbrush.

Do a crayon rubbing of your toothbrush.

Turn your toothbrush into a superhero.

Use technology to create a picture of your toothbrush.

Make your toothbrush out of torn paper.

Make a pattern with your toothbrush.

Draw your toothbrush with the letters from the word *toothbrush*.

Show your toothbrush standing out in a crowd.

Draw your toothbrush from three different perspectives. Label each view.

Draw your toothbrush participating in a historic event.

Draw your toothbrush with one bristle.

Re-create your toothbrush using a specific artist's style.

Re-create your toothbrush using a specific style from art history
(e.g., Abstract Art, Pointillism, Cubism, Surrealism, Expressionism, Action Painting, Impressionism, Realism)

Use the bristles as a paintbrush.

Draw your toothbrush as an animal.

Figure out how much your toothbrush weighs. Use pictures and words to describe how you did it.

Measure your toothbrush in as many ways as possible. Draw and label each measurement.

Compare and contrast your toothbrush drawn with different implements (pen, marker, crayon).

Use as much color as possible.

Show your toothbrush aging over time.

Draw the skeleton of your toothbrush.

Draw things that allude to your toothbrush.

Tell a toothbrush story visually.

Make a toothbrush magazine collage.

Make a toothbrush torn-paper collage.

Paint a toothbrush still life.

Make a Jackson Pollock–style splatter painting with your toothbrush.

Because these prompts were often homework assignments, we wanted to make sure the directions were clear enough for students. We also tried to make the assignments open-ended so we'd get a range of different responses to the same prompt.

We found some unexpected ambiguity in the prompts that led to some interesting discussions about language. For example, we asked students to make a pattern with their toothbrush. Some students interpreted this to mean that they should use their toothbrush as the drawing tool and make a pattern with it. Other students made patterns using their toothbrushes as the pattern element, such as a picture of an upright toothbrush, a sideways toothbrush, an upright toothbrush, a sideways toothbrush . . .). These varied interpretations delighted the students and allowed us to discuss the importance of communication and the limits of language.

It is amazing to see the variety of creative solutions to the same assignment. The interest and enthusiasm expressed for these activities is impressive. The fun and depth of learning quickly becomes apparent in what may at first seem a simplistic activity.

OBJECT JOURNAL SHARING

A journal is a very personal object. It houses the thoughts and feelings of its owner. These ideas are expressed in very individualized ways, often with combinations of symbols and images. Certainly this highly personal aspect of the journal experience needs to be explicitly acknowledged and honored. It's also important for students to know in advance whether their journals are purely private or if they can expect to share them with others. If they are sharing with others, they need to know who the audience is.

Sharing the work challenges students to become more creative with their questions, use their art vocabulary, and come up with new ideas for ways to think about art and math.

Being explicit about how to share journals and how to respond to others' work proved extremely important. Students (and all people) need a safe environment in which to share their creations. Modeling active listening and appropriate remarks helped immensely. We structured the journal sharing so that students responded with compliments, specific positive comments, and questions. We even offered sentence frames.

> For sharing a journal:
>   My favorite page is _____ because _____.
>   On this page I started with _____ and then I _____.
>   This page was challenging because _____.
> For responding to a journal:
>   I like how you _____.
>   How did you make _____?
>   Where did you get the idea for _____?

We also wanted to structure the sharing so that every student did not feel compelled to share every page. Going through every page of every journal could be time-consuming and tedious, so we asked students to think in advance about what they would share. We gave them specific focuses such as these:

> Show one page that you're proud of.
> Show an activity that you learned a lot from.
> Share a page that surprised you.

These prompts helped streamline and focus the sharing. They facilitated conversation. They also allowed the students to do some self-assessment and reflection about their journals before presenting them to others. When using the journal during math time, teachers can ask students to focus on specific concepts or content.

> Show a page where you used measurement.
> Show a page that has different polygons.
> Show a page that required you to do some computation.

When students brought their journals in to share at regular intervals, we witnessed some powerful effects. First, they all remembered to bring them in. Second, they had done all their work, and third, they were very excited about sharing their work. In fact, one day we planned to have students share their toothbrush journals but ran out of time. A near mutiny ensued. Only by promising them we would share the journals first thing the next day did we avoid a full-blown revolt.

OBJECT JOURNALS AND HOMEWORK

Journals focusing on toothbrushes or walnuts offer much potential for interweaving homework assignments throughout the project. Some prompts work better as in-class assignments and others work equally well as homework. Teachers have the best sense of which makes sense for their students and families.

Using journal prompts as homework assignments adds a level of flexibility to the project and invites more family involvement. Notifying and involving families helps keep the homework focused and gives family members an opportunity to participate and learn along with their children. Encourage family members to participate by keeping their own journals and/or asking their children to share theirs. Sharing journals in a family setting offers a fun opportunity to engage in group learning that fosters communication, encourages creativity, and values personal expression. Of course, if teachers prefer to do all the work in class, distributing toothbrushes or walnuts that stay at school works just fine too.

OBJECT JOURNALS IN THE CLASSROOMS

Toothbrush Journals with Third Graders

Marissa Curtis implemented a weeklong toothbrush journal adventure with her third graders. Rather than have them work with their toothbrushes at home, she gave each student a toothbrush in class. This approach addressed concerns about hygiene and homework. She sequenced the activities in the following way:

Day 1: Let students explore their toothbrushes, measure them using standard or nonstandard units, and draw them any way they'd like.

Day 2: Reflect and discuss activities from Day 1. Begin to generate a list of ideas about ways to draw their toothbrushes. Have students choose one idea from the list and use it for that day's journal entry.

Day 3: Add to the class list of drawing ideas. Students rotate through a "Jackson Pollock splatter paint" center where they use their toothbrush to splatter paint on a 12-by-18-inch piece of construction paper. (Splattering inside a deep box will help keep the paint contained.)

Day 4: Students search for geometric shapes in their Jackson Pollock splatter-painted picture and use pencil to outline the shapes. Then they trace over the shapes with a dark marker. Students record (with picture and label) the different shapes they outline in their journals.

Day 5: Use the splatter-painted pictures as a set of task cards. Students look at the shapes, estimate the area in color tiles, measure, and record in their journals. Students can generate extra paintings (they always want to create more).

Extension: Students cut these extra splatter paintings into geometric shapes and use them for collages.

Marissa managed to pull a lot of math from the toothbrush journal experience. The students engaged in artful work and used it as a context for deepening their understanding of measurement and geometry.

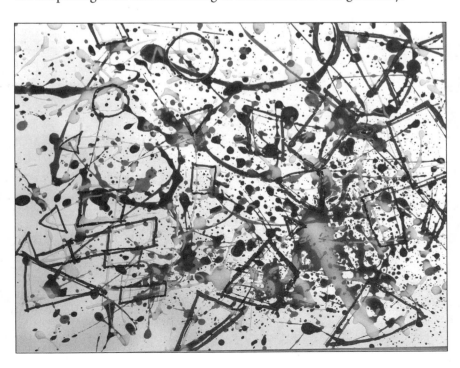

Toothbrush Journals with Deaf and Hard-of-Hearing Students

Jennifer Cole-Regis implemented toothbrush journals with her class of first-through-third-grade D/HH students. The sequence lasted about two weeks. She saw the project as a way to achieve important art and math goals.

The toothbrush journal included a variety of different prompts, some suggested by us and some that Jennifer created herself. The students had been learning about different forms of measurement during math time, so Jennifer thought it was appropriate to have them apply some of the skills from that unit to the toothbrush art. The students used journals made of rectangular pieces of cardstock stapled together. Jennifer had her students do some of the journal assignments in class and others at home.

Jennifer had clearly defined art and math goals for this project. In terms of art, she wanted her students to use art processes and skills with different tools and techniques. She also saw this project as a way for them to use a sketchbook to explore art ideas and to create artwork based on observing an object.

For math Jennifer saw the measurement potential in the toothbrush journal. She structured journal prompts so her students would get practice measuring with nonstandard units. She also wanted them to practice measuring length, width, and weight. The toothbrush journal supplied an excellent context.

She used her own toothbrush journal as a model. She wanted to give students an idea of her expectations and also to show that art can be open-ended and individual. She told students that they would draw their toothbrushes in different ways every day for about two weeks. Students picked out a new toothbrush from a selection to keep at school. Each student had a different color or kind of toothbrush from the others so there was more diversity.

Jennifer carved out time each day to give her students a prompt. She wrote the prompt on the whiteboard inside a rectangle that resembled a page of their journal. After a few days, Jennifer noticed that the students automatically began their daily journal activity after she wrote the prompt. Clearly, the daily activity with its visual element provided a structure for students to take charge of their own work and learning.

She allowed her students to draw their toothbrush in any way they wanted for the first day so they could get a feel for it. For the next two weeks, she assigned topics related to their measurement unit and interspersed other creative activities. Some of the students' artwork amazed her. On one day, students were to measure their toothbrush with nonstandard units such as paper clips and erasers. They had done some nonstandard measuring using paper clips for their math unit so were already familiar with that kind of requirement. She encouraged them to find four different ways to measure their toothbrushes and watched them become creative by using wooden blocks and teddy bears. Another day the students used balance scales to find their toothbrushes' weight in grams. They drew pictures of the scales, the toothbrushes, and the gram weights. They labeled the picture and explained the process.

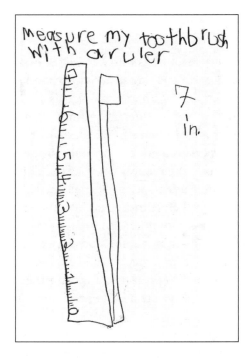

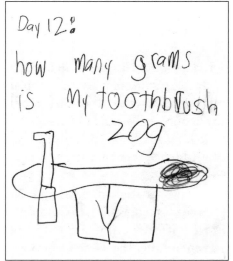

One day during the journal explorations the class took a field trip to the zoo. Upon returning to school, Jennifer had students transform their toothbrushes into an animal they had seen. One student drew his toothbrush as a giraffe, and another drew turtles.

On a daily basis, Jennifer watched her students grow increasingly engaged with drawing their toothbrushes in different ways. She emphasized that art did not need to be perfect. Rather it was a way to express ideas and show understanding. She truly enjoyed watching her students draw or paint their toothbrushes in a variety of ways while applying math skills. She thought her students learned that art is exciting and interesting and easily connected to math. She also delighted in seeing her students appreciate the variety of art produced. The *Blind Contour Portraits* assignment especially reinforced this notion. Jennifer knew her students enjoyed their journal work because almost every day, at least half the students came to her or the aides to proudly show their work with smiles on their faces.

In the future, Jennifer has several more possibilities for continuing or modifying the toothbrush journal. Instead of two weeks, she might consider the possibility of continuing for a month or drawing different objects on a monthly basis. She'd also like to have the students do more of the assignments at home and involve their families more.

Overall, Jennifer was very pleased with the project. Students readily familiarized themselves with the daily journal structure. They completed core math tasks while engaging in creative endeavors that tied together math and art.

A FINAL WORD ABOUT JOURNALS

Although the examples in this chapter focus primarily on toothbrushes and walnuts, we encourage teachers to use journals to focus on other objects as well. The models we've provided merely serve as a window to the possible applications of a math/art journal. Journals offer abundant ways for students to consider the math in art and the art in math. We hope the ideas and samples in this chapter entice teachers and students to creatively incorporate math/art journals in ways that best fit their own creative and mathematical endeavors.

CHAPTER 9

THE CLASSROOM

The classroom provides a rich and relevant array of opportunities for exploration and extrapolation. Teachers and students are literally in the middle of it all, so the connections to sculpture, three-dimensional properties, space, distance, and movement abound. The classroom as a space for art and math gives students the same experiences artists and mathematicians encounter as they make sense of their environment.

Furthermore, the classroom is full of objects, meaning that artists and mathematicians can consider both the physical objects in the classroom and the classroom space itself. Focusing on the classroom can serve as an excellent introduction to the skills and concepts required to combine mathematics and visual art. The classroom might also serve as a culminating study, giving students an opportunity to combine and expand the ideas they have developed through working with various individual objects throughout the year.

One recommendation before embarking on a classroom math/art journey is to keep things consistent. Avoid rearranging the classroom

ACTIVITY	GRADES	NUMBER AND OPERATIONS	ALGEBRA	GEOMETRY	MEASUREMENT	DATA ANALYSIS AND PROBABILITY
Classroom Shape Search	K–2	✓		✓		
Classroom Shape Sorting	K–2	✓				✓
Classroom Polyhedra Hunt	K–2, 3–5			✓		
Clock Maps	1–5				✓	
Classroom Measurements	K–2, 3–5				✓	
Classroom Treasure Map	3–5			✓	✓	
Classroom Movement Map	3–5	✓			✓	
Classroom Quadrilaterals	3–5	✓		✓	✓	
Three-Dimensional Classroom Model	3–5			✓	✓	
The Classroom Museum	3–5	✓	✓	✓	✓	✓

furniture, switching out things posted on walls, or having students change seats while you're doing these activities. It's best to leave the classroom as is, because many of the activities build on one another. It might be confusing or difficult to follow up on an activity if the foundational elements have been moved or changed.

This chapter has four main types of activities. First, we present some ways for students to find and record shapes of objects in the classroom. The next sequence of activities gives students different ways to think about mapping the classroom. The third group of activities focuses on measuring various aspects of the classroom and creating models. The last activity, *Classroom Museum*, challenges students to seek out the mathematics embedded in the classroom and represent these mathematical ideas through posters.

THE CLASSROOM AND THE MATHEMATICS

There's so much math in the classroom that it's almost silly to try to list the possibilities. There are loads of opportunities for counting, grouping, measuring, predicting, sorting, and graphing. We did a sequence of activities focusing on the classroom as a whole and having students think of their space as a math museum. We also offer some other ways to use the classroom and its contents as contexts for significant mathematics.

Using the classroom for measurement makes a lot of sense. Estimation, choosing the right tool, and choosing an appropriate unit all make measurement activities interesting and thought-provoking. Students often lack practice with real measurement because they don't have a lot of measurement activities at home and traditional textbooks relegate measurement to a few pages of practice involving pictures of paper clips and rulers rather than the actual objects. There are tons of things to measure in the classroom, and the measurements can all be verified.

In addition to providing relevant and convenient opportunities to do math, focusing on the classroom for math conveys the message that math is literally all around us. This important message gives students the power and interest to seek out mathematical explanations and solutions for real-world problems. It also reinforces the vital idea that our world is a mathematical wonderland. It's all about how you see it.

THE CLASSROOM AND THE ART CONNECTIONS

The classroom focus may be the most relevant to contemporary directions in the art world today. As noted, our world (and the material in it) is a mathematical (and artistic) wonderland. It's all about how you see it and, as an artist, what you do with it. There are endless ways that artists explore their environment and the materials in it. Artists effectively reflect our world to us using the objects and materials that surround us. Artists help us resee and reexperience our world.

The artists referred to in this chapter devote themselves to the examination and direct experience of objects, materials, and space. Artists consider everything in their environment as potential media for making art. Some choose to create room-sized installations, filling a space with hundreds of thousands of the same object. Some consider our relationship to our environment through the altered perspective of a common object. Others collect and reuse discarded materials from their surroundings to create beautiful new images. These artists know materials and space in a special way. They take ephemera and common materials from our immediate world and tell the important human stories embedded within them. They transform objects and space into experience.

Mark Bradford, from South Central Los Angeles, creates mixed-media works on canvas. *Mixed-media* refers to using a variety of different materials to create art. Bradford uses found materials from the environment (particularly his neighborhood streets) such as bits of foil, string, and paper. He layers, paints, and alters the materials to create a textural and dimensional collage image. The incorporation of actual materials and objects into his large and dynamic canvases create a visceral understanding of place. His works have been described as maps that reflect the spaces and experiences of the city.

Julie Mehretu creates work on canvas somewhere between drawing and painting. Her use of two-dimensional line and shape, which she erases and builds up in multiple layers, depicts large three-dimensional spaces such as cities. Using pathways and symbols to represent connections between people and events, she creates visual maps that trace activities and social networks in a building or urban area. Born in Ethiopia and now living in America, Mehretu calls her work "psycho-geographies." She creates powerful images of world conflict and vivid maps of intense activity that depict place, space, and time on a flat surface.

Tara Donovan uses large quantities of everyday common objects and materials in room-sized installations. She takes huge amounts of a single material such as paper cups, drinking straws, translucent tape, or tooth-picks to build up monumental sculptures. Imagine hundreds of thousands of disposable cups stacked to various heights and arranged on the floor in a 20-by-20-foot square in the middle of an otherwise empty room. Or picture a 4-foot cube made only of toothpicks held together by tension.

Donovan's work, like much Installation Art, is best seen in person. Photographs don't do it full justice. It needs to be experienced. Changing the context or size or number of objects in a space challenges us to reex-amine or reexperience our environment in unexpected ways. We begin to see the space around us very differently because of the way an artist has placed the objects in it. Donovan transforms the most mundane of mate-rials into magical visual worlds.

Sol LeWitt's gallery assistants created the famous "wall drawings" from the artist's instructions and diagrams. LeWitt provided a set of instruc-tions that could be applicable to any size wall. The detailed instructions direct assistants to do such things as "draw a line from a point halfway between the center of the wall and the mid-point of the top to a point halfway between the bottom and the lower right corner." The complex directions resulted in simple and beautiful wall drawings. They visually and verbally represented the artist's ideas for transforming a space.

In a work titled *Material Recovery*, Danica Phelps created charts and graphs of multicolored stripes reflecting data collected from her own life. "I have been writing down everything I do and spend money on every day for about 10 years," she explained. "One red stripe represented each dollar I spent, and one green stripe represented one dollar I earned. There were also grey stripes which represented debt" (Zach Feurer press release, 2008). These wall-sized and intriguing-looking striped charts create a strong visual representation of data about everyday life.

Robert Therrien's artwork almost reveres the everyday object. He takes common household objects and simply changes their scale, using the orig-inal material to create giant replicas. It is an exhilarating and disorienting experience to see a stack of dinner plates or a folding chair large enough to stand under. It is a simple idea, one that can be fully appreciated only in its presence. In one project that lasted seven years, he collected and carefully assembled a room entirely of red objects. His work is at the same time playful and profoundly thought-provoking. His work changes our rela-tionship to the objects and space around us. By changing the context or the scale of a common object he invokes questions that generate reflection on our personal perspective. Is our knowledge of an object (or the world) fixed by our experience? Can our feelings about who we are change based on the objects around us? What happens when we see objects in a completely new way?

One way to visually represent ideas and events on a wall is through the use of posters. Posters can dramatically reflect and affect an environment.

We had students study posters and then create posters to reflect mathematical components of their classroom. Andy Warhol is well known for his many posterlike images of popular American icons and common everyday objects. Some consider him a genius for the way he looked at the everyday objects in his environment and artfully represented them. He generated much controversy in the 1960s art world for his series of paintings and prints of a Campbell's soup can and sculptural reproduction of a Brillo box. For hundreds of years artists painted and drew carefully arranged household objects, typically a vase of flowers or bowl of fruit, but not mass-produced commercial objects. The art world was shocked when Warhol presented the image of a common consumer object as art. He used commercial media such as photography and silk screen, and pioneered the medium of posters as fine art. Today posters are exhibited in museums alongside paintings.

The collage by Shepard Fairey reproduced as a poster for the Barack Obama campaign now hangs in the National Portrait Gallery of the Smithsonian Institution. The move of the poster from street art to the museum is in large part because of the earlier work of Warhol. Warhol is now revered as the father of Pop Art, a blend of graphic, commercial, and fine art, still highly visible in our culture today. His work forces us to consider the objects and space around us as material for artistic consideration.

Classroom Art Vocabulary: balance, collage, Installation Art, mixed-media, pattern, Performance Art, Pop Art, proportion, scale, sculpture, space, symmetry, texture, three-dimensional, two-dimensional

THE CLASSROOM LESSONS

LESSON | # Classroom Shape Search

Grade Level: K–2

Math Content Areas: Number and Operations, Geometry

Math Overview: In this activity young students find counting opportunities through exploring their classroom. As students search for common polygons in their classroom, they become familiar with the names and attributes of the shapes.

Guiding Questions:
Number and Operations
How many can you find?
Geometry
What polygons can you find in the classroom?
How can you tell it's a _____?
Where are they?

Vocabulary: | circle, square, triangle, rectangle, quadrilateral

Materials: | pencils, *Classroom Shape Search* recording sheets (see appendix and CD)

Misty Mudd did a classroom polygon search with her first-grade students. In the beginning she tapped students' prior knowledge of the names of four basic shapes (circle, square, triangle, and rectangle) and had them identify objects in the classroom having those shapes. She pointed out how many sides and corners each shape had. Then she showed them the recording sheet and modeled what they were to do for the activity.

For the exploration Misty gave students the recording sheet and told them to find objects in the classroom and record information about them.

Shapes in the Classroom

Name of Object	Picture of Shape	Name of Shape	Number of Sides	How many are in the classroom?
clock	○	Circle	0 sides	1
student desks	▭	Rectangle	4 sides	20
computer	▭	Rectangle	4 sides	2
glue sticks	○	circle	0 sides	47
poster	▭	Rectangle	4 sides	11
book	▭	Rectangle	4 sides	200
pencil	○	circle	0 sides	99
door	▯	Rectangle	4 sides	2
whiteboard	▱	Square	4 sides	10
CD	○	Circle	0 sides	10

Shapes in the Classroom

Sorting Objects

	Objects With 4 Sides	Objects With 0 Sides
1	desks	Clock
2	Computer	gluesticks
3	poster	Pencil
4	book	cd
5	door	
6	white board	
7		

The students enjoyed the opportunity to explore the classroom. Identifying, distinguishing, and learning to re-create shapes are the basis of learning to draw. This kind of practice in a familiar environment builds awareness and recognition skills that are significant to becoming visually literate.

Finally, in the closing of the lesson, students shared their information. This information became the basis for several follow-up activities that follow.

LESSON

Classroom Shape Sorting

Grade Level: K–2

Math Content Areas: Number and Operations, Data Analysis and Probability

Math Overview: As a follow-up to the *Classroom Shape Search* students sort and classify objects according to their attributes. They combine data they gathered about the polygons they found and use this information to create graphs.

Guiding Questions:

Number and Operations
How many of each shape did you and your partner find?

Data Analysis and Probability
How can you show the different shapes you found?
How can you organize your information?

Vocabulary: circle, square, triangle, rectangle, graph

Materials: completed *Classroom Shape Search* recording sheets from the previous activity, glue, large pieces of construction paper

This activity follows the *Classroom Shape Search*. Once students have identified objects that are various shapes, they sort them and graph them. Students cut their recording sheets apart and make groups of square objects, circular objects, triangular objects, and rectangular objects. For a further challenge, pairs of students can pool their cutout images and create a graph that represents the total number of circles, squares, triangles, and rectangles they found. This pictograph with students' pictures glued onto a larger piece of paper helps young students connect visual representations to numerical data. This visual representation of the data gives them a way to organize and count more easily. Asking questions such as "How many squares did you and your partner find altogether?" or "Did you find more triangles or rectangles?" gives students a visual context for practicing combining and comparing quantities.

This lesson also connects to work artists Danica Phelps and Mark Bradford. Students find their visual cataloging of mundane details and materials quite intriguing. A discussion of what people keep track of and how they represent the data makes the ideas of sorting, collecting, and organizing data both personal and creative.

LESSON

Classroom Polyhedra Hunt

Grade Level: K–2, 3–5

Math Content Area: Geometry

Math Overview: The *Classroom Polyhedra Hunt* gives students practice identifying, comparing, and analyzing the characteristics of three-dimensional shapes. These geometric concepts are reinforced as students build the shapes they find.

Guiding Questions: Which polyhedra can you find in the classroom?
What is the name of each polyhedron?
How many faces, edges, and vertices does each polyhedron have?
How can you create these polyhedra out of clay?

Vocabulary: triangle, square, circle, rectangle, face, edge, vertex, vertices, cone, cylinder, cube, rectangular prism, pyramid, straight, curved

Materials: paper, pencil, *Classroom Polyhedra Hunt* recording sheets (see appendix and CD), modeling clay, toothpicks, paper clips

This activity begins in the same way the *Classroom Shape Search* does. Students brainstorm a list of polyhedra. Both younger and older students find an illustrated chart helpful, because they don't often use these terms.

Once the names and features of the polyhedra are established, students take a walk around the classroom in search of some real examples. They bring a pencil and recording sheet with them, and when they find a polyhedron, they write it on their sheet and attempt to draw a picture of the item. After the search students share their findings. Having them use sentence frames to share their discoveries keeps the emphasis on the features of polyhedra.

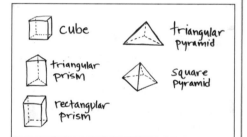

A (item) is a (type of polyhedron).
It has _____ sides.
It has _____ faces.
It has _____ vertices.

Students then choose one of the polyhedra from their recording sheet and attempt to replicate it with modeling clay. Older students might explore more complex polyhedra (octahedron, dodecahedron) and use toothpicks or bent-open paper clips as tools for adding detail to the clay objects. The clay objects can then be shared, sorted, and displayed.

LESSON

Clock Maps

Grade Level: 1–5

Math Content Area: Measurement

Math Overview: *Clock Maps* allow students to consider time and space within their classroom. As students think about their daily schedule and their location throughout the day, they recognize the attributes of time and connect them with specific locations and spatial relationships.

Guiding Questions: What are you doing at different times of the day?
What's the connection between where you are, what you're doing, and what time it is?

Vocabulary: time, clock, location, minute, hour

Materials: *Clock* template (see appendix and CD), pencils, crayons, markers, or colored pencils

Clock Maps employ a common classroom object, the analog clock, as a visual organizing tool for thinking about time and daily schedules. If the daily schedule is posted, use that. If not, brainstorm different activities students do during the day and where and when they do it. Write each activity and the time on the board. From there, distribute the *Clock*

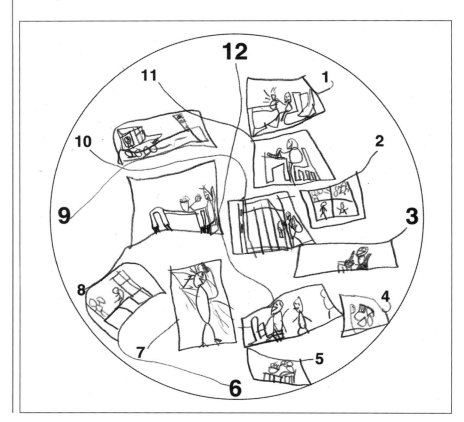

templates to the students. Have them start at the beginning of the day. They need to find the nearest hour on their *Clock* template and create a drawing to show what they do at the start of their day and where they do it. Students continue filling in the details of their daily schedule on their clock faces. The analog circular clock allows for the illustration of twelve hours of activity. Students need to clearly understand their start and end points for this task. We recommend having students begin at 7:00 a.m. and systematically work clockwise until they're back at 7:00 p.m.

Much estimation occurs with this activity, because the clock face is broken into hourly chunks. So for example, if writers' workshop starts at 9:15, students might draw a pencil on their clock face slightly past 9:00. Here students get important practice in representing their ideas in symbols.

Modeling and questioning are immensely important in this activity. Talking through the daily schedule and connecting the times to their locations on the analog clock help students make connections between different representations of time and different parts of the day. Very young students need a lot of modeling and might need a lot of guidance to create their clock maps of a typical day. Older students might tailor their clock maps to the specific activities and places they engage in during the day. Changing the visual format of an art activity (from digital to analog) is a great opportunity for aesthetic problem solving. It challenges students to reflect on the layout of a visual image and how we "read" it.

LESSON Classroom Measurements

Grade Level: K–2, 3–5

Math Content Area: Measurement

Math Overview: This highly adaptable activity uses the classroom as a context for measurement practice. Students encounter important measurement issues such as iteration (use of a unit repeatedly), choosing appropriate units, and using tools to measure length, width, area, and perimeter. Students also develop their estimation skills when encountering large or irregular shapes that are not readily measured.

Guiding Questions:
What can you measure in the classroom?
How can you measure it?
How can you show what you measured?

Vocabulary: measure, ruler, area, linear, perimeter, length, width, height, inch, centimeter, foot, meter

Materials: rulers, tape measures, paper, pencil, paper clips, cubes (other nonstandard measurement tools)

This open-ended exercise gives students practice with measurement. They can focus on linear measurement, area, or perimeter. Younger students benefit from starting with nonstandard units (such as pattern blocks, thumbprints, paper clips, and footsteps). Upper-grade students need practice using and comparing standard units of measure (such as inches and centimeters). Ask students to identify some objects in the classroom that they can measure. Model measuring an item or two, and incorporate the appropriate vocabulary as you describe your process. Ask a student volunteer to come to the front and measure something. Have the rest of the class confirm the process and the accuracy of the measurement. They might even want to measure the classroom as a whole—length, width, height, area, perimeter, or volume. Next send students off to measure three to five items in the classroom. They can work independently or in pairs. To add a visual art element to the measuring experiences, students draw and label the things they measure. This drawing and labeling reinforces the different measurement dimensions and also shows how mathematical information can be communicated through drawings and diagrams. Students can share their drawings as part of the lesson summary. The drawings also work well for a measurement-themed bulletin board.

LESSON

Classroom Treasure Map

Grade Level: 3–5

Math Content Area: Geometry, Measurement

Math Overview: This activity challenges upper-grade students to communicate ideas about location and movement. The math skills involved include creating systems of spatial representation and using coordinate grids to describe location and movement.

Guiding Questions:

Geometry
> How can you make a map of the classroom?
> What shapes and spaces do you need to represent?

Measurement
> How can you show distances between parts of the classroom?
> What types of directions help people find their way?

Vocabulary: location, distance, left, right, forward, backward, above, below, key, scale

Materials: plain or graph paper, pencils, rulers

This activity has art connections to Sol LeWitt's "wall drawings." Have pairs of students decide where to hide an imaginary treasure somewhere in the classroom. The partners then need to create a treasure map with written directions so another pair of students can find the treasure. It helps to have a standard scale to work with. For example, tell students that for the purposes of this mapping activity, one step equals twelve inches. Students record this information on the legend or key at the bottom of their map. Superimposing a coordinate grid on the classroom map may also prove useful in having students describe locations. Using graph paper accomplishes this purpose. Have students assist as you model a brief example on the board.

The treasure map directions combine visual, verbal, symbolic, and quantitative clues. Students need to draw a rough map of the class and designate a starting point for the treasure hunt. Then they need to show how to get from that starting point to the hidden treasure. The use of dotted lines or arrows helps. Writing out directions and telling the map reader how many steps to take and which direction to go help as well. A combination of the two usually proves most helpful.

Other ways to think about and map a place include recording important, memorable, or fun events that happened in various locations. Spatial and verbal skills develop as students describe the relative location of points within the classroom. Learning to read maps and plans is excellent for understanding the relationship between two-dimensional drawings and real-world spaces, and developing skills in spatial awareness, scaling, and measurement.

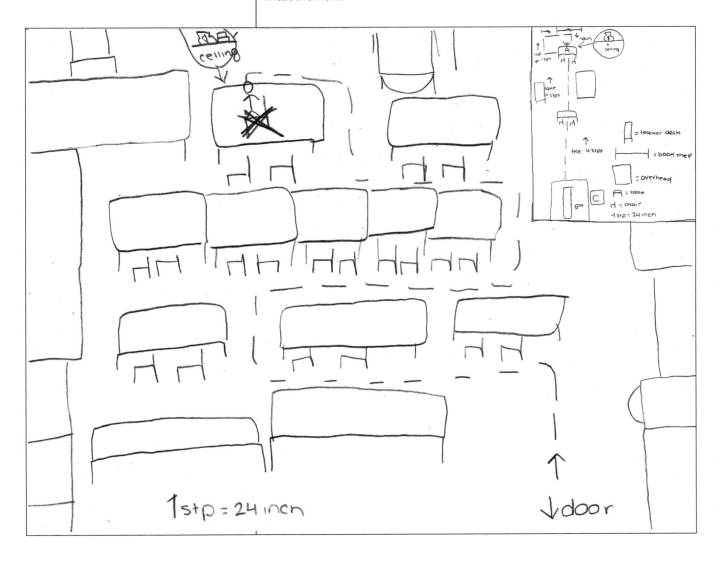

LESSON

Classroom Movement Map

Grade Level: 3–5

Math Content Area: Number and Operations, Measurement

Math Overview: The *Classroom Movement Map* builds on the math skills developed in the *Classroom Treasure Map* activity. Rather than map and describe one location in the classroom, the *Classroom Movement Map* challenges students to spatially represent and calculate the amount of movement they log in the classroom over a period of time. Students use a geometric model to solve problems in the areas of measurement and computational estimation.

Guiding Questions:
Number and Operations
About how far do you walk each day in the classroom?
Measurement
What paths do you take to move around the classroom?
How can you show the paths on a map?

Vocabulary: distance, linear, measure

Materials: paper, pencils, markers or highlighters

This activity requires students to consider their movement through the space of the classroom. Combining concepts of location, time, and distance the *Classroom Movement Maps* require students to stretch their abilities to visually represent mathematical ideas. This activity is a perfect place to introduce the work of Julie Mehretu and analyze how she represents time, space, and activity in one plane.

Students begin by sketching a map of the classroom. They then think about when they move in the room and how they get from one place to another. They use this information to draw their pathways throughout the day.

Color-coding the pathways makes the movement map more legible and provides more information about the individual's movements. Students can color the paths they take before recess in one color, the ones between recess and lunch another color, and the ones after lunch a third color. The colors allow viewers to see how much movement happens at different times of the day and where the activities occur. Also challenge the students to find ways to show how long they stay in each location.

There are numerous measurement and computation challenges that arise from the movement maps. Students can measure the length of their steps and then use the maps to estimate how far they walk around the classroom each day. They can also compile their distance data to find out how far the whole class walks around the room in a day. They might use their daily movement data to estimate how long it takes them to walk a mile in the classroom. They can also estimate the number of steps they take in their classroom each day, week, or month. For a bigger computation challenge students can combine all their steps and estimate how many miles they walk as a class in a week or month.

LESSON

Classroom Quadrilaterals

Grade Level: 3–5

Math Content Areas: Number and Operations, Geometry, Measurement

Math Overview: This activity allows students to consider the plane surfaces of their classroom and the different quadrilaterals resting on the planes. Students use geometric vocabulary and measurement skills to create a representation of the quadrilaterals' location on the plane. Students also explore an area model for fractions.

Guiding Questions:

Number and Operations
What fraction of the wall space is each quadrilateral?

Geometry
What are the different quadrilaterals on the walls?

Measurement
What is the area of each quadrilateral?

Vocabulary: quadrilateral, square, rectangle, parallelogram, rhombus, angle, vertex, side, area, perimeter

Materials: 12-by-18-inch black construction paper, colored construction paper, glue, rulers, scissors, pencils

Classroom Quadrilaterals give students a chance to explore measurement and fractions. Students choose one large plane of the classroom: a wall, the ceiling, or the floor. They draw a sketch of that plane and all the quadrilaterals that reside on it. Then they estimate each small quadrilateral as a fraction of the larger plane it's on. The estimates can be based on rough eyeball measuring, or students can actually find the areas of the various planes and compare the ratios.

Have students create a diagram that shows all the rectangles on the plane in their relative positions and explains how the fraction estimates were made. To expand the visual element, students can transfer their sketches to construction paper. They can measure and cut out the quadrilaterals from different-colored construction paper or from magazine pages and glue them onto a larger sheet of black construction paper. These quadrilateral collages are striking abstract representations of a basic and often overlooked classroom element. Understanding how to organize visual elements is important in all art, and using quadrilaterals is the perfect place to start.

LESSON | Three-Dimensional Classroom Model

Grade Level: 3–5

Math Content Area: Geometry, Measurement

Math Overview: This activity entails building three-dimensional geometric models. Students begin by analyzing the two-dimensional planes of the classroom's walls and floor. From there they measure the size and distance between objects on each plane. To create the classroom model they must address issues of proportion, scale, linear measurement, and spatial reasoning.

Guiding Questions:

Geometry
> What is the shape of our classroom?
> How can our classroom be broken down into shapes and parts of shapes?

Measurement
> What are the dimensions of the walls and floor?
> How does the size of the _____ compare to the size of _____?
> How tall is the door compared with the height of the classroom?

Vocabulary: model, similar, scale, proportion, two-dimensional, three-dimensional

Materials: tagboard, paper, graph paper, scissors, tape, clay

Doing the *Classroom Quadrilaterals* activity before embarking on the classroom model helps to scaffold this task. Students' prior experience focusing on one plane of the class will transfer to the more complex task of combining the planes of walls and the floor.

Students begin by exploring the dimensions of the classroom—length, width, area, and height. They then need to decide on a scale. The scale could be standardized, such as one inch equals one foot, or it could emerge from less formal questions such as "If your thumb is the size of a person, how big would the desks be? How long would the room be? How high would the ceiling be?"

Emphasize that the model students make will be much small than the actual classroom but that it needs to be proportional or similar to the actual classroom. If the classroom is squarish in shape, the model needs to be squarish as well. The decision about scale accuracy depends on the students' grade level and background knowledge. If they have the background, they can work with a standard scale and try to be as accurate as possible. Younger, less experienced students will estimate and try to get things to be reasonably close to the proportions of the room and its contents.

Students work in groups with the tagboard serving as the external classroom structure. Students need to estimate the floor dimensions and wall height and mark the tagboard accordingly.

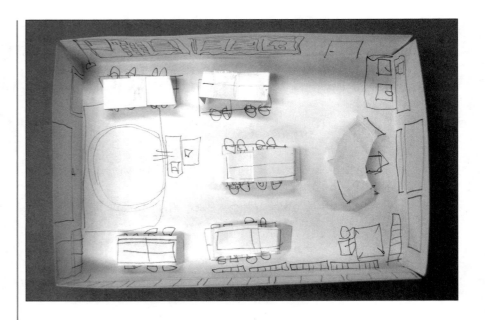

From there students use pencil to sketch the locations of various items in the classroom (such as desks, chairs, bookshelves, doors, and windows). After the classroom sketch is complete, students cut and fold up the sides of the tagboard to create the floor and walls of the classroom.

Showing students actual blueprints is a useful and interesting way to introduce this activity. They will learn the difference between a "plan view" (a drawing looking straight down, like a bird's-eye view) and an "elevation" (a drawing looking straight across when standing in front). Most schools have a school site plan somewhere, used for exiting and fire drills. Often local reprographics companies or architectural firms have discarded sets of plans they are more than willing to contribute.

Once the tagboard template is complete, students create scaled versions of the various items they sketched in the classroom. They can use folded paper, tape, and scissors to create the classroom furniture. Other options include modeling clay, toothpicks, craft sticks, packing peanuts, wooden blocks, centimeter cubes, or other materials available in the classroom.

Regardless of the materials, students work to create proportional, scaled models of their classroom and the objects within it.

LESSON | The Classroom Museum

Grade Level: | 3–5

Math Content Area: | All

Math Overview: | *The Classroom Museum* project engages students in a broad survey of mathematics in their surroundings. Rather than focus on one particular content area, students investigate their classroom and search for evidence of mathematics throughout. In doing so students accomplish wide-ranging mathematical goals such as problem solving, communication, and making connections.

Guiding Questions: What can we count or measure in the classroom?
What geometry ideas can we see in the classroom?
What patterns can you find in the classroom?
How can we share the math we find in the classroom?

Vocabulary: pattern, geometry, museum, number, measurement, size

Materials: *Math Museum Poster Planning* sheets (see appendix and CD), poster paper (12-by-18-inch construction paper or larger drawing paper), rulers, pencils, black markers, crayons, sample posters

Mathematician Glen Whitney inspired this project. Whitney's love of math prompted him to envision a math museum. Although the museum itself does not yet exist, Whitney uses the entire island of Manhattan as a prototype. He leads tours of the city and points out the mathematical elements of things as varied as traffic lights, building design, and supermarket checkout counters. If he can turn a city into a math museum, we figured we'd try the same thing with a classroom.

Day 1

We launched the investigation by telling Tina Rasori's fifth graders about Glen Whitney. We shared that he loved math and saw math everywhere he went—even in New York City. We then asked the students to imagine Glen coming to their classroom. Which parts of the classroom might have math in them? At first students focused solely on math-related aspects of the room: math books, charts about math, things with numbers on them. Then they started thinking more broadly and saw that the table arrangements had math, the books had math, and pretty much anything had some aspect of shape, pattern, number, or size.

We asked about shapes in the classroom. Students pointed out several, and we recorded them on the board. We continued by having them talk in pairs about patterns in the room and numbers in the room. We recorded these ideas on the board as well. A student mentioned that lots of things in the room had size and could be measured, so we added a size/measurement category.

We used a lot of partner talk throughout the discussion. We wanted to make sure students had a good handle on the concept of searching for math within their classroom and had enough vocabulary and ideas to work on their own. This partner talk proved especially helpful to the many English language learners in the room. It helped them connect the terms, the concepts, and the objects to the physical space of their classroom.

From here we showed the students a simple half-page recording sheet. We instructed them to find a partner and pick an area of the classroom to search for math.

We kept the structure as simple and open-ended as possible so students would have the freedom to explore whichever part of the classroom they wanted and to focus on math areas that were accessible and interesting to them.

Students worked on their investigations for a while, and then we called them together to do some sharing. They had discovered many mathematical aspects of their classroom. They expressed enthusiasm for the task and its open-endedness: "I liked that you can know some things that you didn't know before." "I liked that you can choose what to see and look at." "I like going around the room and looking for numbers."

The math ideas they generated in this investigation served as the jumping-off point for the next day's work.

Day 2

During our next class session with them, we began with a review of what the students had done on our previous visit. We asked if they had noticed any other math in the classroom since then, and a few students shared.

We reminded the students of Glen Whitney and told them that his dream was to create a math museum. We were going to use this idea to start turning the classroom into a math museum. We'd use all the information they had discovered during the previous class and turn it into posters that could be displayed around the room. That way, anyone who visited the classroom could learn about the math that was in the room.

We wanted to push the idea of posters and design to encourage students to create thoughtful and effective products. We showed some sample posters and asked students what they thought the posters were for and how they knew.

We asked students questions such as these:

What do you notice?
How do the posters show you what's important?
How do the posters get your attention?

They had many insights. They noted the pictures, the font, the size of different images, and the colors. These ideas built a framework for the posters that they designed and created. We connected the students' responses to some basic elements of design. We talked about layout and how the size and location of different items within the poster show the viewer what's important and guides the eye around the poster. We also pointed out the use of symmetry, balance, and patterns in posters. With these features in mind, we told students that they were going to create their own posters for the classroom math museum.

To further support their process Tina modeled the process of making a poster. She used the bookshelves as an example. She prompted the students to generate a list of mathematical elements of the bookshelves and recorded their ideas on the board. From there she asked the students questions to help them understand the important aspects of creating a poster. She drew a rectangle around the ideas written on the board.

"So," she began, "how does this look? Should I just copy all your ideas on a piece of poster paper and then I'm done?"

"No!" was the unanimous response from the students.

"What should I do to make the poster more interesting?" Tina asked.

"Try putting some pictures on it," one student suggested.

"Maybe you can draw the bookshelves and show the math in different colors," another student added.

"Also, you can make the important ideas bigger so you don't need to write so much. You can just show it," contributed another student.

As the students made these suggestions, Tina created a draft poster on the board and incorporated their ideas. As the poster sketch took shape, students saw the effective elements and continued to make suggestions. They had many ideas, and we pushed to have them incorporate the concepts of size, balance, and layout. It was crucial to have them understand that posters communicate primarily through images and symbols—their size, location, intensity, color, and repetition. Words play a subordinate role. When it was clear the students had many ideas and strategies for their poster designs, Tina sent them off to work.

As students worked on their posters, we circulated, offering support and asking questions to keep them focused on communicating the mathematical ideas in as clear a way as possible. We found questions like these helpful:

What is your poster about?
How are you going to show the important ideas?
What will people learn from looking at your poster?

After the students had had some time to work on their posters, we stopped them to check in. We asked how things were going, what they liked about the job, and what was challenging. We also refocused them on the math by asking them where the math was in their posters and how they were showing it. This discussion helped students focus further on the task and gave them more ideas and approaches to the work. We then let them get back to their individual posters.

The final products impressed everyone. Students' posters featured such topics as bookshelves, wall charts, computers, and tables. With the posters displayed throughout the room, the classroom indeed looked and felt like a math museum.

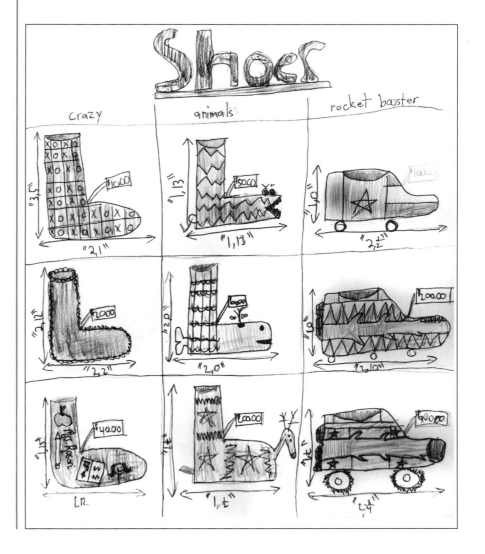

AFTERWORD

Little did we imagine that some innocent conversations about math and art would turn into a book. And little did we imagine that this book would come together with the help and support of so many colleagues who enthusiastically joined the conversation and opened their classrooms (and their minds) to the possibilities that combining elementary math and contemporary art provided.

What problem are you working on? What kind of materials might help you? In what ways might you organize the information? How can you communicate your thinking to others? These are the types of questions we ask our students when they are working on math problems. These are also the types of questions mathematicians and artists ask themselves as they approach their work. By asking these questions of ourselves and our students, we can go on growing as teachers, learners, mathematicians, and artists.

As we persist in exploring art and math connections, we'll be able to bring math and art alive in our classrooms. Whether approaching an activity through its math content or introducing our students to an intriguing artist or art idea, we continue to find exciting and creative ways to use math to support art and art to support math.

And using art to teach math gives us direct access to the creative process. As Wolk (2008) implores us, "Let students create things. People like to make stuff. Having control of our work and using our minds and hands to create something original give us a tremendous sense of agency. There is a special pride in bringing an original idea to fruition. It empowers us and encourages us." (11).

We encourage teachers to consider how they might effectively educate all students, not just for "the test" but for life as contributing and engaged citizens. We can give our children interesting, relevant, contextual opportunities to explore their world, their creativity, and their mathematical understanding through activities that integrate visual arts and math. We hope this book serves not only as a teacher resource, but as an invitation to continue to explore, innovate, and create.

BIBLIOGRAPHY

Asthon, Dore. 1992. *Noguchi East and West.* Berkeley: University of California Press.

Berger, John. 1972. *Ways of Seeing.* London: Penguin Books.

Burns, Marilyn. 2007. *About Teaching Mathematics: A K–8 Resource.* 3rd ed. Sausalito, CA: Math Solutions.

Christo and Jeanne-Claude. http://christojeanneclaude.net.

Common Core State Standards. 2010. http://www.corestandards.org.

Dewey, John. 1934. *Art as Experience.* New York: Perigree Books.

Eisner, Elliot. 1998. *The Kind of Schools We Need.* Portsmouth, NH: Heinemann.

Friedman, Thomas. 2010. *New York Times* (OpEd), August 4.

Fuller, R. Buckminster, and Kiyoshi Kuromiya. 1992. *Cosmography: A Posthumous Scenario for the Future of Humanity.* New York: Macmillan.

Goldberg, Merryl. 2005. *Integrating the Arts: An Approach to Teaching and Learning in Multicultural and Multilingual Settings.* Needham Heights, MA: Allyn and Bacon.

Grandin, Temple. 2009. *Animals Make Us Human.* New York: Mariner Books.

Greene, Maxine. 2001. *Variations on a Blue Guitar.* New York: Teachers College Press.

Hiebert, James et al. 1997. *Making Sense: Teaching and Learning Mathematics with Understanding.* Portsmouth, NH: Heinemann.

Lin, Maya. 2000. *Boundaries.* New York: Simon and Schuster.

Lockhart, Paul. 2009. *A Mathematician's Lament: How Schools Cheat Us Out of Our Most Fascinating and Imaginative Art Form.* New York: Bellevue Literary Press.

Lomas Garza, Carmen. 2000. *In My Family/En Mi Familia.* San Francisco: Children's Book Press.

———. 2003. *Magic Windows/Ventanas Magicas.* San Francisco: Children's Book Press.

———. 2005. *Family Pictures/Cuadros de Familia.* San Francisco: Children's Book Press.

National Assessment of Educational Progress (NAEP). 2009. http://nces.ed.gov/nationsreportcard/mathematics/.

National Center for Education Statistics. 2007. Trends in International Math and Science Study (TIMSS). http://nces.ed.gov/timss/.

National Council of Teachers of Mathematics. 1989. *Curriculum and Evaluation Standards for School Mathematics.* Reston, VA: NCTM.

National Council of Teachers of Mathematics. 2000. *Principles and Standards for School Mathematics.* Reston, VA: NCTM.

National Council of Teachers of Mathematics. 2006. *Curriculum Focal Points for Prekindergarten Through Grade 8 Mathematics: A Quest for Coherence.* Reston, VA: NCTM.

National Council of Teachers of Mathematics. 2009. *Guiding Principles for Mathematics Curriculum and Assessment.* Reston, VA: NCTM.

National Visual Arts Association. 1994. National Visual Arts Standards. http://artsedge.kennedy-center.org/teach/standards/introduction.cfm.

Paumgarten, Nick. 2009. "Mathhattan." *The New Yorker,* August 3.

Pink, Daniel H. 2006. *A Whole New Mind.* New York: Penguin Group.

Schmidt, William H. 2004. "A Vision for School Mathematics." *Educational Leadership,* February.

Schnapp, Jeffrey T. 2008. "Art in Schools Inspires Tomorrow's Creative Thinkers." http://www.edutopia.org/arts-role-creative-thinking.

Skorton, David. 2007. "The Arts Are Essential." Adapted by the author from an address given at the forum "Transforming Arts Teaching: The Role of Higher Education," sponsored by the Dana Foundation, New York.

Stigler, James, and James Hiebert. 2004. "Improving Mathematics Teaching." *Educational Leadership,* February.

Wilde, Judith, and Richard Wilde. 1991. *Visual Literacy.* New York: Watson-Guptill.

Wolk, Steven. 2008. "Joy." *Educational Leadership,* September.

Zach Feuer Gallery. 2008. "Material Recovery" press release. New York.

ART EDUCATION REFERENCES

Americans for the Arts
http://www.americansforthearts.org/
Arts Education Partnership
http://aep-arts.org/
Arts for Learning
http://www.arts4learning.org/
California Alliance for Arts Education
http://www.artsed411.org/index.aspx
The Center for Arts Education
http://www.cae-nyc.org/
The Kennedy Center ArtsEdge
http://artsedge.kennedy-center.org/educators.aspx
National Art Education Association
http://www.naea-reston.org
National Endowment for the Arts
http://www.arts.gov/index.html
National Gallery of Art
http://www.nga.gov/education/classroom/index.mhtm
National Standards—Princeton Online
http://www.princetonol.com/groups/iad/Files/standards.htm

PBS Art:21
    http://www.pbs.org/art21/index.html
TED Seminars
    http://www.ted.com/search?q=art&x=0&y=0
Visual Arts—Content Standards (California State Board of Education)
    http://www.cde.ca.gov/be/st/ss/vamain.asp
Visual Art Vocabulary Sources
    http://www.artlex.com
    http://www.cde.ca.gov/be/st/ss/vamain.asp
    http://www.artcyclopedia.com

DIGITAL LINKS/ONLINE COLLECTIONS

The Artchive
    http://artchive.com/
ArtCyclopedia
    http://www.artcyclopedia.com/
Art History Resources on the Web
    http://witcombe.sbc.edu/ARTHLinks.html
Art Images for College Teaching
    http://arthist.cla.umn.edu/aict/html/index.html
The British Museum—Explore/World Cultures
    http://www.britishmuseum.org/explore/world_cultures.aspx
WorldImages—California State University
    http://worldimages.sjsu.edu/
Crown Point Press
    http://www.crownpoint.com/
The Getty—Conducting Research
    http://www.getty.edu/research/conducting_research/
Harvard University Library Visual Information Access
    http://via.lib.harvard.edu/via/deliver/home?_collection=via
Los Angeles County Museum of Art
    http://www.lacma.org/art/CollectionsOverview.aspx
Musée de Louvre
    http://www.louvre.fr/llv/commun/home.jsp?bmLocale=en
MacArthur Foundation
    http://www.macfound.org/site/c.lkLXJ8MQKrH/b.3599935/
    k.66CA/MacArthur_Foundation_Home.htm
Metropolitan Museum of Art
    http://www.metmuseum.org/toah/
Musée d'Orsay
    http://www.musee-orsay.fr/en/collections/works-in-focus/home.html
Museum of Arts and Design
    http://www.madmuseum.org/
Museum of Modern Art
    http://www.moma.org/explore/collection/index
National Gallery of Art
    http://www.nga.gov/

National Museum of Women in the Arts
    http://www.nmwa.org/collection/
Peabody Museum of Archaeology and Ethnology at Harvard University
    http://www.peabody.harvard.edu/
Smithsonian Institution
    http://www.si.edu/
Stuart Collection—University of California, San Diego
    http://stuartcollection.ucsd.edu/StuartCollection/index.htm
Studio Museum in Harlem
    http://www.studiomuseum.org/
Tate Museum
    http://www.tate.org.uk/
UCLA and SPARC César Chávez Digital/Mural Lab
    http://sparcmurals.org/ucla/index.php?option=com_
    frontpage&Itemid=1

ARTIST CHART

The following chart shows a complete list of artists referenced in this book. The icons next to each artist's name indicate which chapters/objects they are connected to. This chart also serves as a springboard for teachers who choose to approach the activities via the art and artist, in addition to the mathematics.

We have also included links to individual artists' Web sites on the CD that accompanies the book. We hope that this chart, the icons, and the CD will provide teachers with easy access to information about the artists. We encourage teachers to explore the resources and to introduce interesting and noteworthy artists to their students.

THE FACE

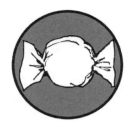

FOOD

GRIDS AND
GRAPH PAPER

THE ROCK

PAPER

THE SHOE

THE FLAG

THE JOURNAL

THE CLASSROOM

ARTISTS

Agnes Martin

Josef Albers

Anni Albers

Sol LeWitt

Roy Lichtenstein

Piet Mondrian

Faith Ringgold

Carl Andre

Eleanor Antin

Elizabeth Murray

René Magritte

Robert Rauschenberg

Chuck Close

Pablo Picasso

Georges Braque

Frida Kahlo

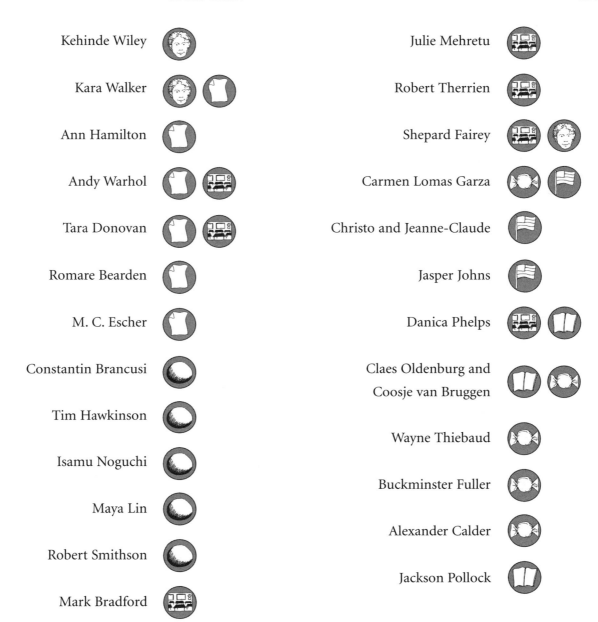

REPRODUCIBLE FORMS

DISPROPORTIONATE PORTRAITS

Name _____ Partner's Name _____

Use a ruler to measure your partner's face. Record measurements below.

	Length	Width
Face		
Eye		
Nose		
Ear		
Mouth		
Chin		
Forehead		
Cheek		

Pick one feature to double _____ New length =   New Width =

Pick one feature to halve _____ New length =   New Width =

Use the measurements to draw and cut out the features for your partner's portrait collage.

CEREALSCAPES RECORDING SHEET

Name _____

_____ **and** _____ _____ **scape**

I used _____ plain circles.

I used _____ colored circles.

I used _____ squares.

I used _____ wheels.

I used _____ other shapes.

Altogether I used _____ pieces of cereal.

I found the total by _____

_____

_____

_____

_____

_____

POLYGON TEMPLATE

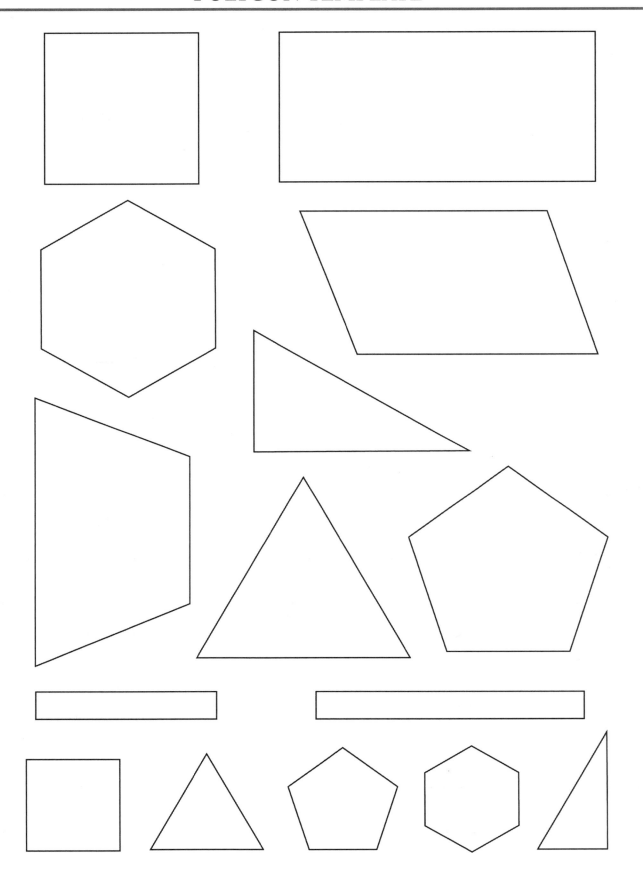

POLYHEDRA FOOD SCULPTURES

Name _____

Name of Polyhedron	Picture	Number of Faces	Number of Vertices	Number of Edges

PASTA AND PIPE-CLEANER PLAYGROUNDS

Name _____

I made a _____ .

Here is a picture:

[ ]

It is _____ centimeters high.

It is _____ centimeters long.

It is _____ centimeters wide.

I used _____ pipe cleaners.

I used _____ pieces of pasta. Here's how I figured it out:

[ ]

CANDY BLOCK SCULPTURES

Name _____

I made a _____ .

Here is a picture:

```

```

It is _____ cm long.

It is _____ cm wide.

It is _____ cm tall.

I used about _____ pieces of candy. I made this estimate because

_____

_____

_____

TEN-BY-TEN GRID

HUNDREDS CHART GRID

1	2	3	4	5	6	7	8	9	10
11	12	13	14	15	16	17	18	19	20
21	22	23	24	25	26	27	28	29	30
31	32	33	34	35	36	37	38	39	40
41	42	43	44	45	46	47	48	49	50
51	52	53	54	55	56	57	58	59	60
61	62	63	64	65	66	67	68	69	70
71	72	73	74	75	76	77	78	79	80
81	82	83	84	85	86	87	88	89	90
91	92	93	94	95	96	97	98	99	100

GRIDS A

GRIDS B

OBJECT LESSONS

DECIMAL CHART GRID

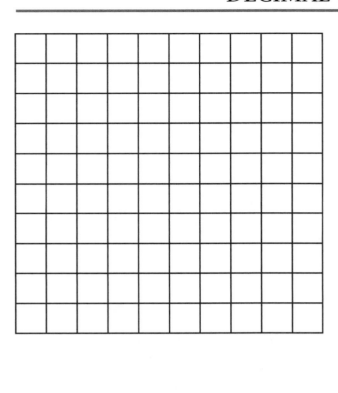

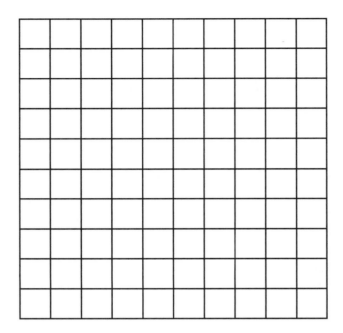

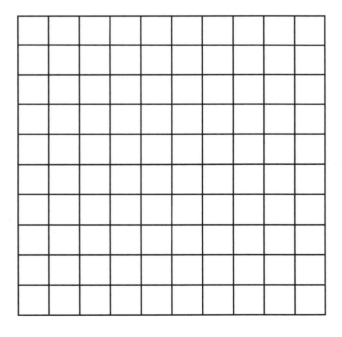

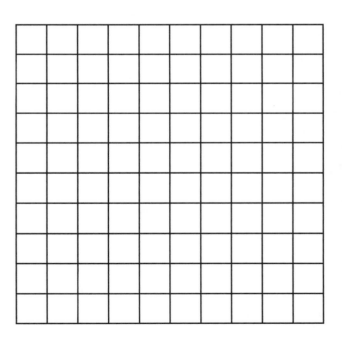

ROCK GARDEN

Name _____

Estimate how many rocks will cover each rock cutout in your garden. Use the table below to record them in order from smallest to largest.

Rock Cutout	Estimate	Actual	Difference
1			
2			
3			
4			
5			
6			

The total number of rocks in my rock garden is _____.

Here is how I found the total:

ROCK GARDEN TEMPLATE

CAVE PAINTING PLANNING SHEET

Name _____

1. Write the equation:

2. Tell a story to match your equation.

3. Draw a picture to show your story.

PAPER FOLDING CHALLENGE

Name _____

# of Folds	# of Shapes	Picture	Shape Name	Initials

Show your table to a partner. See if your partner can re-create the shapes you folded. Have your partner initial each shape that he or she copies successfully.

Pick your favorite square to copy on a 6-by-6-inch square. Use a black marker to outline each shape within your square and decorate inside the shapes.

PAPER BEAD RECORDING SHEET

Name _____   Partner's Name _____

My pattern number is 2 3 4 6.

My pattern number color is RED YELLOW ORANGE BLUE GREEN.

The other colors I'm going to use are RED YELLOW ORANGE BLUE GREEN.

1	2	3	4	5	6	7	8	9	10	11	12

I notice _____

_____

_____

_____

_____

_____

_____

_____

_____

PAPER BAG SCULPTURES

Name _____

Use the recording sheet below to measure your original bag and estimate the measurements for your paper bag sculpture.

	Original Bag	Sculpture Compared with Original Bag	Sculpture Estimate
Length			
Width			
Height			
Surface Area			
Volume			

What did you learn?

What was challenging about this activity?

On the back of this paper draw your paper bag sculpture.

ALL ABOUT MY SHOE

Name _____ Partner's Name _____

Measure it:

	Estimate	Actual
Length		
Width		
Height		
Volume		
Surface Area		
Sole Area		

Describe it:
(Line, Shape, Color, Pattern, Texture)

My shoe has _____ and _____ .

I see _____ .

The shapes on my shoe are _____ and _____ .

I also notice _____

_____

Trace it.
Redesign it.
Name it.
Cut it out.

SHOE RUBBING

Name _____   **Partner's Name** _____

On the back of this page use words, numbers, and pictures to describe the patterns you see.

FLAG TEMPLATE 1

FLAG TEMPLATE 2

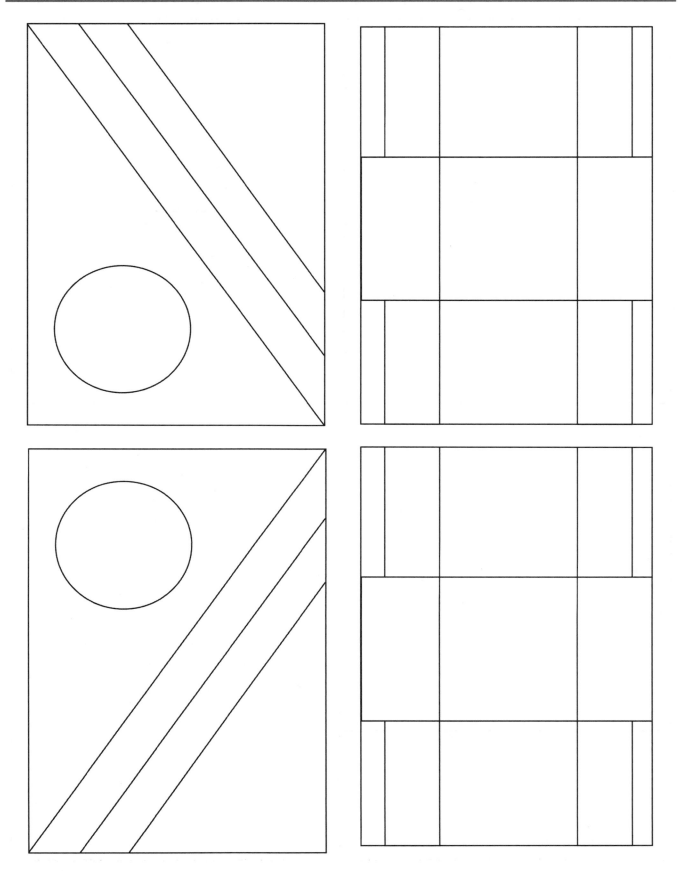

FLAG TEMPLATE 3

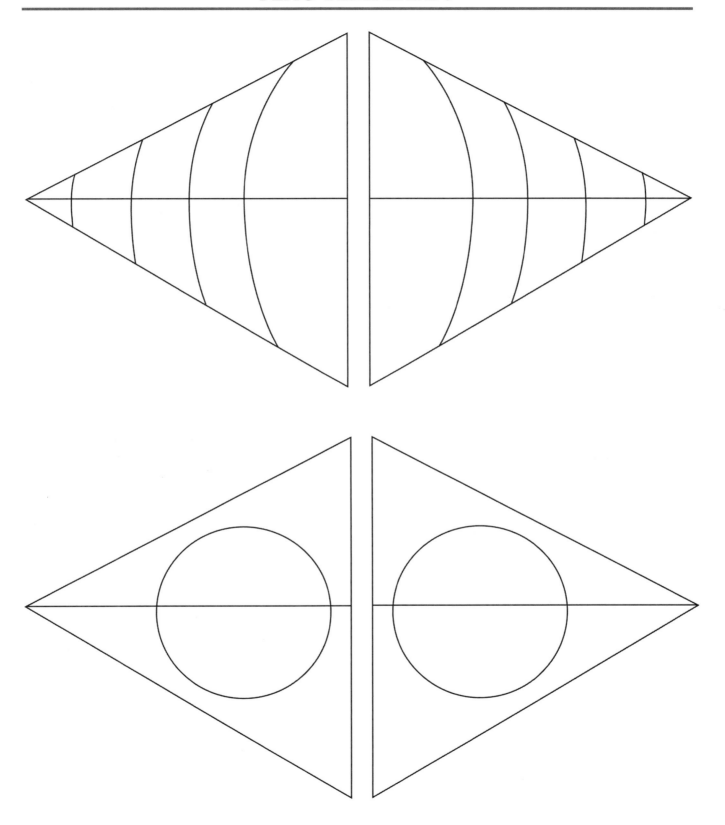

PRIMARY COLORS SPINNER

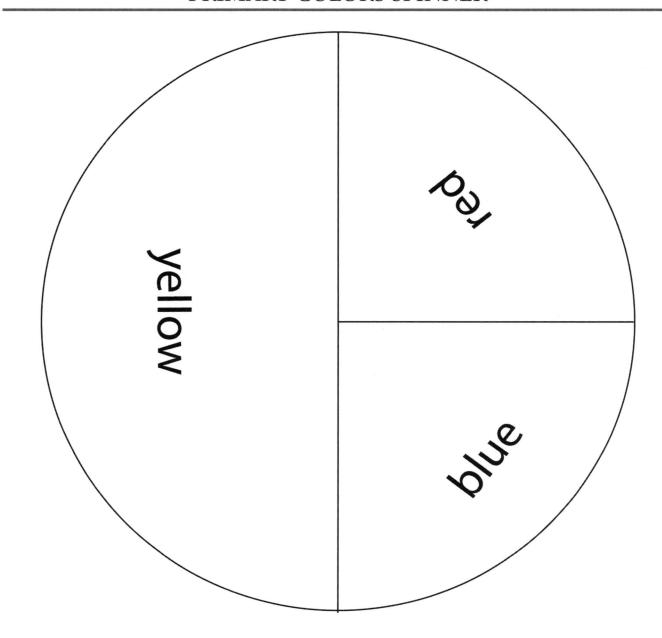

FLAG SPINNERS

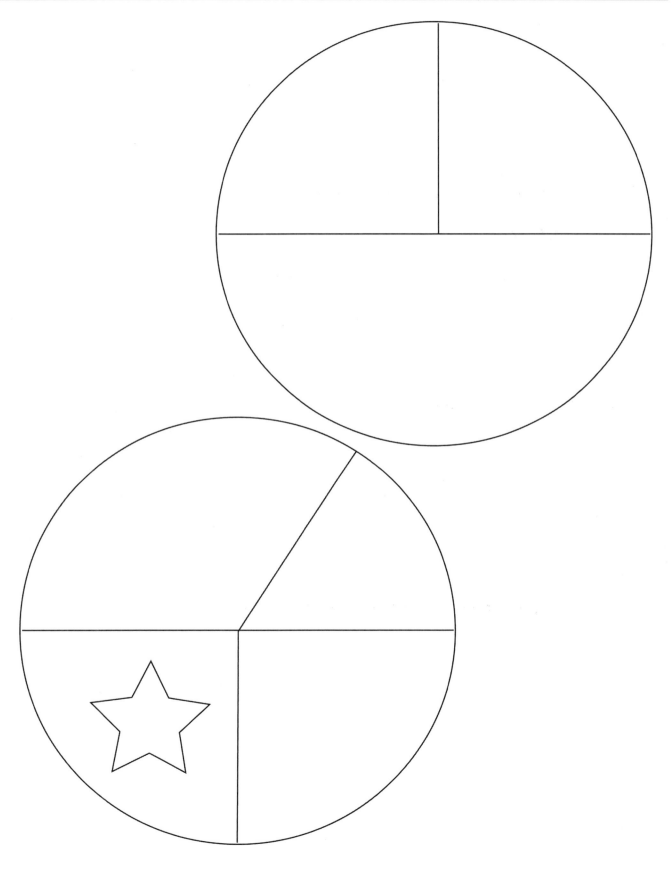

SPIN A FLAG

Name

1. Look at the spinner. Describe each color on the spinner as a fraction.

2. Make some predictions about your flag colors.

   It is likely that my flag will _____ because _____

   _____ .

   It is unlikely that my flag will _____ because _____

   _____ .

   It is impossible for my flag _____ because _____

   _____ .

3. Use the spinner to design and color your flag.

4. Tell how your predictions compare with your actual flag.

NAUTICAL INITIAL FLAG

Name _____ **Initials** _____ _____

1. Use fractions to estimate the colors of your first initial.

   White: Black:

   Blue: Red:

   Yellow:

2. Use fractions to estimate the colors of your second initial.

   White: Black:

   Blue: Red:

   Yellow:

3. On the back explain how you estimated your fractions. Use words, numbers, and/or pictures.

   Colors used:

   I figured it out by

   I used the most _____

   I used the least _____

   About half of my name is _____

   About one-fourth of my name is _____

Extensions: Add the fractions together or do whole name.

CLASSROOM SHAPE SEARCH

Name _____

Name of Object	Picture of Shape	Name of Shape	Number of Sides	How Many Are in the Classroom?
clock				
student desks				
computer				
glue sticks				
poster				
pencil				
door				
whiteboard				
CD				

CLASSROOM POLYHEDRA HUNT

Name _____

Polyhedron Name	Polyhedron Picture	Classroom Example	Number of Faces	Number of Edges	Number of Vertices
Cube					
Rectangular Prism					
Triangular Prism					
Rectangular Pyramid					
Triangular Pyramid					

CLOCK

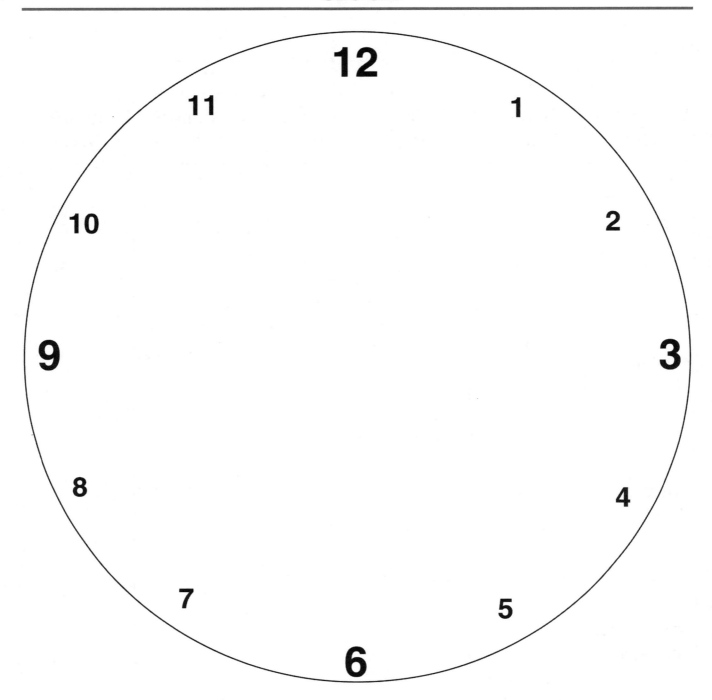

MATH MUSEUM POSTER PLANNING

Name _____ Partner's Name _____

What is your poster about?

Choose 3 colors for your poster.

_____ _____ _____

What shapes, images, or pictures will you use?

What words will you use?

What numbers will you use?

What is the title of your poster?

Sketch a plan for your poster on the back of this page. Think carefully about the important message of your poster and how you're going to show the message. Decide where you want to put things and how big you want to make them.

Your poster needs to
    have words, numbers, and pictures;
    have a title;
    use different sizes to show what's important;
    include a pattern somewhere;
    use letters between 1 inch and 5 inches tall.

INDEX